Offa and the
Mercian Wars

Offa and the Mercian Wars

The Rise and Fall of the First Great English Kingdom

Chris Peers

Pen & Sword
MILITARY

First published in Great Britain in 2012
and reprinted in this format in 2017 by
PEN & SWORD MILITARY
An imprint of
Pen & Sword Books Ltd
47 Church Street
Barnsley, South Yorkshire
S70 2AS

ISBN 978 1 52671 150 2

A CIP catalogue record for this book is
available from the British Library

Typeset in 11/13.5 Palatino by Concept, Huddersfield, West Yorkshire

Printed and bound in Malta by Gutenberg Press Ltd.

Pen & Sword Books Ltd incorporates the Imprints of Aviation, Atlas,
Family History, Fiction, Maritime, Military, Discovery, Politics, History,
Archaeology, Select, Wharncliffe Local History, Wharncliffe True Crime,
Military Classics, Wharncliffe Transport, Leo Cooper, The Praetorian Press,
Remember When, Seaforth Publishing and Frontline Publishing.

For a complete list of Pen & Sword titles please contact
PEN & SWORD BOOKS LIMITED
47 Church Street, Barnsley, South Yorkshire, S70 2AS, England
E-mail: enquiries@pen-and-sword.co.uk
Website: www.pen-and-sword.co.uk

Contents

List of Illustrations

Maps

Plates

1. Roman Icknield Street in Sutton Coldfield Park
2. Roman settlement at Wall
3. Excavated Roman ruins at Wall
4. The façade of Lichfield Cathedral
5. Sculpture of Penda on the front of Lichfield Cathedral
6. Offa depicted on the facade of Lichfield Cathedral
7. Saint Chad's Well at Stowe, near Lichfield
8. A decorated hilt from a reproduction of the Sutton Hoo king's sword
9. A reproduction Anglo-Saxon sword of around the ninth century
10. A reconstruction of the eighth-century Coppergate helmet
11. Another view of the reconstructed Coppergate helmet
12. A reproduction spangenhelm
13. The church of All Saints at Brixworth, Northamptonshire
14. The tower at Brixworth
15. The River Tame at Tamworth
16. Tamworth Castle
17. The River Ouse at Bedford
18. Section of Offa's Dyke near Craignant, north of Oswestry
19. Section of eastern slope of Offa's Dyke
20. Steep western approach to the top of Offa's Dyke

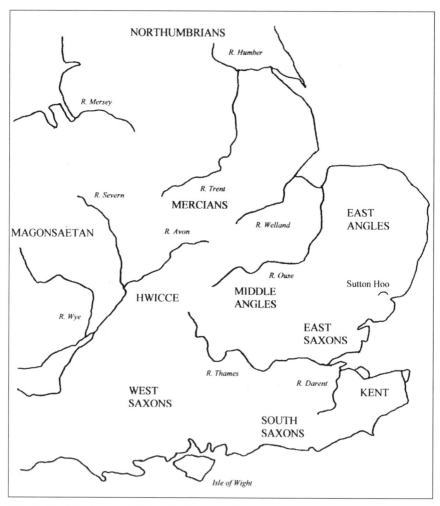

Map 1. The Mercians and their neighbours, c. AD 600.

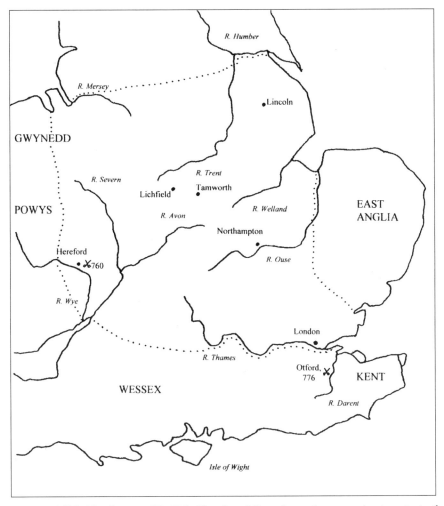

Map 2. Offa's kingdom, c. AD 790. The dotted line shows the approximate extent of Offa's direct rule. All of the named surrounding kingdoms recognised his overlordship at least temporarily.

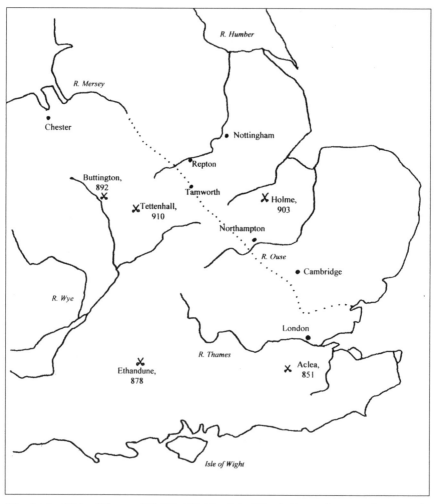

Map 3. *The Viking Wars, c. AD 850–920. The dotted line indicates the approximate south-western boundary of Danish settlement.*

Prologue

Canterbury in the summer of 785 was a city not so much conquered by force of arms as stunned into submission. The ancient capital of the Anglo-Saxon kingdom of Kent, the seat of an archbishop, and a place which had already been Christian for almost two centuries, this was the most sophisticated settlement in England – one of the few places where those who could afford them had access to luxuries imported from the European mainland. From here emissaries went south to Rome and even Constantinople, and traders arrived from overseas with the products of exotic lands. But it was no longer in Canterbury that real power resided: a fact which was now being brought home to the inhabitants in the most uncompromising terms. The hundreds of dust-stained warriors who urged their weary horses through the streets on this ominous morning may have seemed strange and rustic to the men of Kent, but they were received in awestruck silence. They might have been mocked in secret as half-pagan savages, but their grim demeanour – and the reputation of the man who rode at their head – ensured that not a hand was raised in resistance. These were the Mercians from the heart of England, a wild frontier region famed as the school of warriors. Clad in coats of mail and iron helmets, bearing glittering spears and swords ornamented with the loot from countless victories, they were the mightiest army that England had yet seen. Their leader was the famous Offa, for nearly thirty years king of Mercia, and overlord of the neighbouring kingdoms as far as his raiding armies could reach. Now, at the height of his power, no one could be found to dispute his self-proclaimed title of 'king of all England'.

Nine years previously the Mercians had met the men of Kent in battle at Otford on the River Darent, and after a day of dreadful slaughter on both sides Offa had retired, not defeated, but unable to obtain a victory decisive enough to secure his supply lines as he advanced further into hostile territory. Since then Kent had enjoyed a precarious independence under a local ruler named Ecgberht, but the shadow of the Mercian armies, though they were temporarily distracted on other frontiers, had never been entirely dispelled. Now Ecgberht was dead and Offa was here in his place, having led his elite mounted warriors on a ride of 200 miles from the Mercian heartland to surprise the men of Kent before their new ruler could raise an army, or even open negotiations. We have no eyewitness report of his arrival in Canterbury, but Notker's account of Offa's contemporary Charlemagne at Pavia in 773 may give us an idea of the impact the unexpected appearance of such an army could have. Rank after rank of horsemen advanced on Pavia, coalescing into a 'battle line of iron', in the centre of which rode Charlemagne, armoured in mail and holding aloft his sword. The defenders, we are told, panicked or fainted at the sight, the terrified citizens crying out in despair, 'iron, iron everywhere!' Before the summer was out Offa would be holding court and issuing proclamations as if Kent was his by right, its ancient royal dynasty reduced to the status of vassals. So who was this man who, 1,000 years before Napoleon, could strike down kingdoms by his mere presence? Whence did he derive this power, and how did his successors lose it so completely that the name of Offa has been almost forgotten? This is the story of the Mercian kings, their victories and defeats, and the rise and fall of the first great English kingdom.

Introduction

As taught in English schools for most of the last two centuries, and to a lesser extent still in the popular imagination, 'English history' begins, paradoxically, with the Norman Conquest of 1066. Apart from the Victorians' exaggerated admiration for empire builders such as the Normans, there are more understandable reasons for this disregard of the preceding centuries, an age which in reality saw the true creation of the English state. One reason is the scarcity of physical remains, for whereas places such as Greece, Italy and even southern France can show a more or less continuous sequence of buildings, aqueducts and other relics stretching from Roman times up to the present, in England there is very little to be seen from the period between the abandonment of the Roman villas at the end of the fourth century AD and the appearance of the first stone castles at the beginning of the twelfth. Documentary sources show a similar pattern, because English people of the fifth and sixth centuries were on the whole illiterate, and when their voice does start to be heard they are writing in a strange-looking language which at first glance bears little resemblance to the French-influenced English of the later Middle Ages. We do not even call them English: they are the 'Anglo-Saxons', a name which emphasises their supposed alien origin, and the period in which they lived is popularly referred to as the 'Dark Ages', a label which almost removes it from history altogether into a world of myth and mystery, where any wild speculation or crank theory can flourish, and often does.

However, the country which the Normans conquered already had a long history. Domesday Book, compiled only twenty years after the conquest, describes a settled land of mostly prosperous villages, organised into shires and hundreds under a tight hierarchy of ownership, loyalty and obligation, their territories carefully arranged to provide each community with access to ploughland, pasture, woodland and other resources. The Normans did not create this arrangement. They owed it to the true owners of the land, whose efforts had brought it into the orbit of Roman Christianity after the chaos following the collapse of Roman secular power, and who had saved it from the Vikings, and turned it into probably the best governed and most productive kingdom in Europe. They had also produced some of the most celebrated artistic achievements of the early Middle Ages. Some of these, such as the illuminated Lindisfarne Gospels and the treasures of Sutton Hoo, have long been popular icons of Anglo-Saxon culture, but others are only now coming to light. In 2003 restoration work at Lichfield Cathedral in Staffordshire unearthed the 'Lichfield Angel', a magnificent eighth-century limestone sculpture now recognised to be of 'European importance' ('The Lichfield Angel and the Saint Chad Gospels', booklet, Chapter of Lichfield Cathedral, 2005). And six years later, only a few miles outside Lichfield, the buried war gear of the 'Staffordshire Hoard' emerged to challenge again our concept of the 'Dark Ages' with its exquisite decoration of gold and semi-precious stones. What is particularly interesting about these recent discoveries is their location in the English Midlands, in what was then the 'forgotten kingdom' of Mercia. (The counties into which England was traditionally divided, incidentally, provide a useful guide to locating the places mentioned in this book, but they were not yet in existence in the Midlands in the time of the Mercian kings. They were introduced during the tenth century when the rulers of Wessex brought the area under their control after the Viking invasions.) For of the four main kingdoms into which Anglo-Saxon England was once divided, Mercia has always been regarded as the least interesting from a historical as well as a cultural point of view. Northumbria, whose heartland was along the north-east coast, had the great monasteries which produced the Lindisfarne Gospels and other symbols of the 'Northumbrian renaissance', as well as the influential historical work of Bede. East Anglia has the burial ground of its kings at Sutton Hoo, while Wessex, in the south, was the kingdom of Alfred the Great, the best-known pre-conquest English monarch, whose dynasty accomplished the defeat of the Vikings and the unification of the country in the tenth century.

However, as we are now coming to appreciate, Mercia was no backwater. In fact, in the seventh, eighth and early ninth centuries AD, before Wessex rose to its position of pre-eminence, it was the Mercian kings who dominated their neighbours and first earned the title of 'kings of England'. Men such as Penda, Wulfhere, Aethelbald and the greatest of them all, Offa, whose name has always been associated with the famous 'Offa's Dyke' along the Welsh border, and who received from a learned contemporary the description 'the glory of Britain'. Their rise was not a peaceful one, and battlefields across half of England, mostly now lost, were soaked in the blood of the Mercians and their enemies during their three centuries of glory. This book attempts to tell the story of how and why they achieved their victories and survived their defeats. Luckily the sources for this period are more extensive than they at first appear, and the last few decades have seen archaeologists and historians make dramatic progress towards putting it on a firmly historical footing. The most important narrative source for the early part of our period is Bede's *A History of the English Church and People*, which was written in Latin around the year 731. The 'Venerable' Bede, as he has become known, was a monk who spent almost all his life in the monasteries at Jarrow and Monkwearmouth, in what was then the kingdom of Northumbria. He produced numerous erudite works, of which this history is by far the best known. As the title suggests, its primary concern is the conversion of the English to Christianity and the subsequent development of the church, but Bede also includes much information on political events and military campaigns, especially where these illuminate the careers of the early English saints. Despite the inclusion of miracle stories which the modern reader often finds difficult to take seriously, his book is a significant work of scholarship by the standards of the time, and he is often careful to identify his sources. Nevertheless his perspective is strongly pro-Northumbrian, and he is generally indifferent or even hostile to Mercia, which, for most of the century before he wrote, was Northumbria's traditional enemy. It is particularly unfortunate from our point of view that Bede died in 735 and did not live to record the career of Offa, although notes added to his manuscript after his death by an anonymous continuator do refer briefly to Offa's rise to power.

The other indispensable source is of course the Anglo-Saxon Chronicle – or rather Chronicles, because this compilation survives in several versions, written at different locations, whose relationship to one another is the subject of constant scholarly debate. Apart from the main chronicles associated with Winchester, Worcester, Abingdon, Peterborough and Canterbury, passages from what were apparently once independent works such as the Chronicle of Aethelweard, and the so-called Mercian Register covering the years 902 to 924, have been copied into some of the surviving versions. In order to avoid unnecessary confusion I have usually referred to all these sources as the Anglo-Saxon Chronicle. This is not unreasonable as they do follow each other very closely in most of the entries with which we are concerned, and they clearly derive from a common source. This source was probably first drawn up during the reign of King Alfred, was written in a West Saxon dialect of Old English, and mainly reflected the concerns of Alfred's own kingdom of Wessex. It was kept up to date more or less continuously from Alfred's time until the twelfth century. Like Bede, the Chronicle generally regards affairs in Mercia as of little consequence, and sometimes it displays a distinct political bias. But also like Bede, it is often the only source we have for the events it describes. The Chronicle gives a fairly detailed narrative of events from the end of the ninth century onwards, and is especially valuable for the Viking Wars of that period, but before that it seldom contains more than brief notices of the main events of each year. Many of these are evidently derived from Bede, and others apparently from notes inserted into tables produced by monks for the calculation of Easter.

6

This source has often been used as evidence for the earliest period of Anglo-Saxon England, the supposed 'invasions' of the late fifth century, but here it is particularly unreliable, and its focus is almost exclusively on the West Saxons who were traditionally believed to have founded the kingdom of Wessex.

The *Life of King Alfred* written by the subject's chaplain, Asser, complements the Chronicle for the reign of its subject, but again is inevitably West Saxon in its outlook and concerns. Two other well-known works of early English literature belong to myth as much as to history, but they do provide us with an unrivalled picture of the 'sharp end' of Anglo-Saxon warfare. The first is the epic poem *Beowulf*. This survives only in one late copy, but from internal evidence it has been deduced that it was first written down sometime in the century or so following the birth of Bede in 682 (Stenton). It is also thought that, although the present version is written in the West Saxon dialect, the original was composed in that part of the country which traditionally was settled not by Saxons but by Angles – probably, in other words, in Northumbria or Mercia. The poem may therefore be contemporary with the Mercian kings Aethelred, Aethelbald or Offa, or even have been composed at their courts. Its subject matter is not historical, but it powerfully evokes the world of the Anglo-Saxon warrior in the age of transition from paganism to Christianity. The other great English war poem recounts the exploits of Earl Byrhtnoth and his men at the Battle of Maldon in 991. Although dating from two centuries after the zenith of Mercian power, it describes weapons and tactics very similar to those which must have been used by Offa's armies, and presents a detailed account, if not of how a battle actually was fought, at least of how the noble classes believed it should have been. It is reproduced in full, in Old English and in translation, in Pollington (2001).

The notorious polemic entitled *On the Ruin of Britain*, written in the sixth century by a British monk named Gildas, is almost invariably the first point of reference for any study of early Anglo-Saxon England, but from our point of view it is of limited relevance and dubious reliability. The name of Nennius, a Welsh writer of the late eighth or ninth century, is traditionally attached to two more

7

useful works which he may have edited rather than compiled personally: the *Historia Brittonum* or 'History of the Britons', and the 'Welsh Annals'. Nennius' stated intention was to reconstruct the history of the 'Britons', or non-English inhabitants of the island, which had been shamefully neglected by their own scholars. He remarks ruefully that their failure to keep proper records has forced him to rely heavily on English sources, so he can hardly be regarded as an independent source himself. However, he does provide some useful additional information, mainly from a Welsh perspective. Nennius is better known nowadays as the first historian to describe the career of the legendary King Arthur. A selection of early Welsh poems, notably the eulogies for Cadwallon and Cynddylan, two of Mercia's allies, shed a further faint light on affairs in central England in the lifetimes of their heroes.

I have also been unable to resist some of the contributions made by Henry of Huntingdon, whose *History of the English People* was written at Lincoln early in the twelfth century. Henry seems to have consciously intended to bring Bede up to date, and obviously relied on him for much of his early material. However, he does include additional details, especially in his battle accounts, which are written in his characteristically lively and entertaining style. Some of these accounts probably derive from his own imagination, but others contain hints that they might preserve material from other sources now lost, the 'chronicles preserved in ancient libraries' which the Bishop of Lincoln advised him to consult. Another reason for not disregarding Henry is his location in the East Midlands, which put him in a better position than either Bede or the West Saxon annalists for recording oral traditions relevant to Mercian history. Several other writers of the post-Norman Conquest period dealt with the early Anglo-Saxons, and may, like Henry, have had independent sources to which we no longer have access. They include Simeon of Durham, Florence of Worcester, Roger of Wendover, William of Malmesbury, Matthew Paris, and the author of the fourteenth-century *Flowers of History*; the latter is traditionally ascribed to Matthew of Westminster and I have retained this attribution here, even though Matthew himself is now believed by many to be a fictional character.

Many writers on the subject of Anglo-Saxon warfare have relied heavily on analogy with Scandinavian sources, especially the Viking sagas. This is understandable because of the shortage of detailed accounts of English battles, and because the Scandinavian material does seem to come from a very similar warrior culture to that described in *Beowulf*, for example. Weapons were almost identical, and it is logical to assume that so were the methods of using them. However, while acknowledging that these sources can sometimes shed light on our subject, I have tried not to lean too heavily on them. They are, after all, at two removes from the world of the Mercian kings, having been written down in distant lands several centuries after the events they purport to describe.

Other sources which can illuminate the Mercian Wars in passing include the published laws of several Anglo-Saxon kings (none of them, unfortunately, Mercian), and the biographies of saints, not all of whom led entirely peaceful lives. Reference will also be made to the surviving 'charters' of the period from the eighth century onwards, which record grants of land made by kings and others in authority, often to ecclesiastical houses. These rather dry documents are of interest for two main reasons. Firstly, they record the names and often the titles of the parties, and so can show where a certain person was at a particular time and how he wished to style himself. The location of Offa's 'palace' at Tamworth, for example, is deduced not from a specific statement in the narrative sources but from the frequency with which he issued charters from that town. Similarly, documents in which Offa grants land in other kingdoms, such as Kent, provide us with a guide to the extent of his power as well as hinting at his presence on military campaigns. Many charters also define the extent of the territory they grant by describing a perambulation of its boundaries, and these have enabled scholars to reconstruct the appearance of the countryside and the frequency of woods, roads and other features.

In addition to written documents, we also have the huge and constantly growing supply of material provided by archaeologists,

9

which has revolutionised our understanding of this and other periods, as well as providing ammunition for debate on all sorts of questions which we would once have thought lost in obscurity. At the same time textual criticism has cast doubt on the reliability of what we thought were solid facts, written down once and for all in 'black and white'. Nevertheless, despite recent attempts to bring the two disciplines closer together, writers on this period remain divided into two camps: those who use archaeology mainly to illuminate the documentary sources, and those for whom excavated material provides the only real 'hard' evidence, in contrast to the subjective and unreliable texts. I have tried to steer a middle course between these extremes, but two considerations have pushed me in the direction of the first camp. I am not trained as an archaeologist, and in any case the real interest of military history often lies in matters with which excavated artefacts alone cannot help us. What bring it to life are the names and motivations of the commanders, the strategy and tactics of the campaigns, and the deeds of the heroes. All too often, in a period as remote as this one, these have to be guessed. The words 'probably' and 'perhaps' appear far too often in these pages, for which I apologise. But that is probably better than giving a false impression of certainty, and surely better than discarding the written sources altogether, for all their weaknesses.

Rulers of Mercia, c. AD 600–874

	Reign	Relationship to previous rulers
Cearl	c. 600	
Penda	626–654	Unknown
Peada	654–656	Son of Penda
Wulfhere	658–675	Son of Penda
Aethelred	675–704	Son of Penda
Coenred	704–709	Son of Wulfhere
Ceolred	709–716	Son of Aethelred
Aethelbald	716–757	Grandson of Penda's brother Eowa
Beornred	757	Unknown
Offa	757–796	Great-great-grandson of Eowa
Ecgfrith	796	Son of Offa
Coenwulf	796–821	Descendant of Penda's brother Cenwalh
Ceolwulf I	821–823	Brother of Coenwulf
Beornwulf	823–826	Unknown
Ludeca	826–827	Unknown
Wiglaf	827–840	Unknown
Beorhtwulf	840–852	Unknown
Burhred	852–874	Unknown
Ceolwulf II	874–?	Unknown

Chapter 1
Offa's Country

The country which was to become the kingdom of Mercia occupies the approximate centre of England. It can be envisaged as a rough rectangle with its corners on the sea at the mouths of four rivers – clockwise from the south-west, the Severn, Mersey, Humber and Thames. In a great loop across the northern half of this region flows a fifth river, the Trent, along whose banks was situated the original core of the kingdom, 'the land that was first called Mercia'. Running first southwards through what is now the county of Staffordshire, the Trent flows from west to east a few miles north of Lichfield and Tamworth – respectively the religious and civil centres of eighth-century Mercia – then north-east via Nottingham to join the Humber. On either side of the Middle Trent Valley is high ground – the Peak District of Derbyshire in the north, and the Birmingham Plateau to the south, now named after the region's major city, which was an insignificant village in Anglo-Saxon times. The valley itself, however, contains some of the best agricultural land to be found in Europe. South and east of the Middle Trent is a wide swathe of rich lowland bounded by the swamps of the East Anglian Fens on the east, and on the south-east by the forested Chiltern Hills, almost a hundred miles from Tamworth. This was the territory of the Middle Angles, a closely related people who seem never to have had a kingdom of their own, most of whom had already come under Mercian control by the time our records begin. Beyond the Chilterns is London, at the mouth of the Thames, which, running across southern England from west to east, formed in historic times the boundary between the Mercians and the West Saxons. In the opposite direction, looking west from the edge of the Birmingham Plateau on a good day, you can see the Welsh hills sixty miles away. Between the two uplands the River Severn flows southwards towards the Irish Sea. East of its lower reaches lay the kingdom of the Hwicce, and between the Middle Severn and the hills of Wales a people called the Magonsaetan; both these groups were at least partly British rather than Anglo-Saxon in their culture and had once been independent kingdoms in their own right, but like the Middle Angles they had already become a part of the Mercian power bloc by the time our written sources begin.

This was the landscape that was to produce the first great English kingdom. It is not a big country by Continental standards, and despite its location in the centre of the island of Britain no part of it is more than seventy miles from the sea. Its rivers are also on a modest scale – you can throw a stone across the Trent at Newark, only fifty miles from its mouth – and none of its hills much exceed 1,000 feet above sea level. However, the maritime climate is relatively warm for its latitude, and the west winds provide reliable rainfall. People had been living in this land ever since the end of the Ice Age – essentially the same people, because modern DNA studies suggest that the old notion of successive waves of immigration was greatly exaggerated and that most of the modern inhabitants of Britain are the direct descendants of the original pioneers of the Stone Age. It is likely that all the primeval forest which once covered the land had been cleared for fields and pasture long before Mercia came into being, and most of the villages on the map today were already in existence in some form by the beginning of our period.

This was by no means the Dark Age wilderness of popular imagination. It would, however, seem very alien to a modern observer. Most shocking would be the way in which people lived for much of the time on the edge of subsistence, with famine and epidemic disease on a scale now seldom encountered outside Africa. Bede tells how in Sussex in the late seventh century a prolonged drought brought a famine so severe that people committed suicide by throwing themselves from cliffs rather than face a lingering death from starvation.

13

Around the same time Saint Chad, one of the first Mercian bishops, died along with most of his colleagues from an outbreak of epidemic disease. And yet somehow the land produced large enough surpluses of food and population to sustain a wealthy warrior class and continually repair the damage inflicted by its incessant wars.

The Landscape

In order to understand the nature of military campaigning in the Mercian Age it is necessary to build up a picture of the sort of country over which these campaigns took place. It is likely that people were very aware of the distinction between wild and cultivated landscapes – a distinction which drives the plot in *Beowulf*, for example, in which the halls of men are constantly threatened by monsters from the woods and marshes. However, even in the seventh and eighth centuries there can have been little if any true wilderness in England, except perhaps in the Fens of East Anglia where Saint Guthlac sought refuge from the world amidst the demon-haunted marshes.

The bears, wild cattle and bison which Offa's contemporary, the Frankish emperor Charlemagne, hunted in the forests beyond the Rhine had long ago disappeared from the British Isles, probably by the end of the Bronze Age. Wolves were still widespread in Anglo-Saxon times, though perhaps even then not that common, and there are hints that their activities may sometimes have been a political issue, or even a cause of conflict. According to William of Malmesbury, in the tenth century the English king Edgar imposed a tribute on the princes of North Wales of 300 wolf skins annually; this was paid for three years, but ceased after that because the Welsh could find no more wolves in their territory. No doubt the pelts had some value in trade, but historians have always considered this a rather strange demand when Edgar could have insisted on cattle, silver or other more obviously useful goods. It has been suggested that the king was interested in the pelts as clothing for his troops, or even a kind of uniform for his bodyguard, but we have no other evidence for Anglo-Saxon warriors dressed in wolf skins. Another

possible explanation is that the mountainous Welsh terrain provided a refuge for the predators which had already been driven
out of most of lowland England. The Welsh herdsmen, who raised
mainly cattle and horses, may not have considered the wolves to
be enough of a threat to be worth hunting down, whereas to the
English, dependent on their more vulnerable flocks of sheep, their
presence would have been intolerable. Perhaps Edgar's subjects
had complained of the damage done by 'Welsh' wolves raiding
across the border in search of easy prey, obliging him to force his
neighbours to address the problem. It is even possible that similar
considerations had applied two centuries earlier in the reign of Offa,
whose kingdom already relied heavily on the wool trade, and that a
secondary purpose of his famous dyke (discussed in more detail
on pages 136 to 140) was the control of four-legged raiders as well as
human ones.

Most of the settlements identified by archaeologists from the
period between AD 500 and 700 were situated on or near river banks,
more than half of them being within 500 metres of a permanent
source of water. However, the villages were less permanent than
in later centuries, and many of them were apparently moved or
abandoned – either temporarily or permanently – at some time
during the seventh and eighth centuries. This may of course have
been the result of political insecurity and chronic warfare, but
there is also some evidence that the climate around this time
was relatively unstable, with alternating droughts and floods
and several severe winters (Arnold). For example the Anglo-Saxon
Chronicle mentions a 'great mortality of birds' in 671, presumably
the result of extreme cold, as well as the notorious 'big winter' of 763.
Archaeological discoveries suggest that sheep were the commonest
livestock, followed by cattle. The latter were used not just for milk
and meat but to pull ploughs, as horses were very rare in agricultural communities. Most agricultural land was used for grain
crops, mainly barley and oats, with wheaten bread probably
remaining a scarce luxury food.

As discussed below (pages 28 to 29), modern research has dis-
proved the theory that the Anglo-Saxons took over an abandoned

15

and mostly forested landscape, and it has been estimated that the proportion of wooded country in the first millennium AD was already less than 20 per cent (Rackham). It was, however, much less evenly distributed than it is today. In the later Middle Ages there seems to have been a dramatic contrast between what Professor Rackham calls 'Ancient Countryside', which retained its pre-Roman and Roman patchwork of small fields, pasturelands, hedgerows and woods, and the 'Planned Countryside' characterised by huge, open arable fields, lacking natural obstacles and parcelled out among its cultivators in parallel and more or less regular strips. The true 'open field' system was probably a development of the tenth and eleventh centuries, but Rackham has detected signs that the difference between the two landscapes may go back much further. Place names referring to woods and clearings are much more common in Ancient Countryside, for example, and the features mentioned as boundary markers in charters from the eighth century onwards show a similar pattern. Especially in the Planned Countryside most woods were probably managed for timber, though less thoroughly than in Roman times, and so were by no means impassable to large bodies of men (Brooks). There is evidence that they were routinely surrounded by banks and ditches, probably intended to keep live-stock from straying and wild pigs out of the fields, and no doubt some of these banks have subsequently been mistaken for military earthworks. On the other hand they could have been useful as instant defensive lines for outnumbered armies. Contemporary written sources do not appear to mention this tactic, however, and on the whole it seems that wooded areas were regarded as unsuitable for military operations.

Rackham suggests that the contrast between the two types of landscape may have been as dramatic as that between the Normandy 'bocage' and the open plains of Champagne in France today. If so, it must have had a significant influence on the conduct of warfare. The 'open country' formed a rough triangle with its points on the English coast at Great Yarmouth in Norfolk, Portland Bill in Dorset, and the mouth of the River Tees in North Yorkshire. Its boundaries were of course irregular, following local vagaries of terrain, and there were no doubt isolated patches of woodland within it. Conversely the 'wooded country' was typically a mixture of clearings, coppices and lightly wooded pasture. There may have been a more or less continuous belt of such close terrain running south-westwards across the country from the Humber to the Lower Severn, incorporating what were to become the Forests of Sherwood and Arden, and the escarpment of the Cotswolds further south (Hooke, 1985). This must have been a considerable barrier to armies moving between the kingdoms of Wessex and the Hwicce.

It is also noteworthy that the Mercian heartland around Tamworth lies very close to the boundary between Rackham's two landscapes. To the west and south-west lay the Forest of Arden and the hills, heaths and scattered hamlets of Cannock Chase and the Birmingham Plateau, while marching eastwards a Mercian army would soon have found itself in a rolling agricultural countryside with long lines of sight and little or no cover. Perhaps this partly explains the concentration of recorded battles in the corridor east of the southern Pennines and along the Berkshire and Wiltshire Downs, where the terrain lends itself to rapid manoeuvre and armies would have found it relatively easy to locate each other.

Rivers were the most important strategic features in the land-scape, and are referred to repeatedly in the campaign accounts which survive. Guy Halsall (in Hawkes) has shown that the great majority of the identifiable battle sites of the Mercian Age are located either at ancient burial mounds or similar well-known sites of obvious cultural significance, or at river crossings. It is quite likely, as he suggests, that the former were chosen as pre-arranged rendezvous, but it is less certain that this also applied to the river crossings. Given that settlements, and therefore supplies of food, were concentrated near rivers, and that fording them must often have been a protracted operation, it seems probable that any army in the field would have spent more time near river banks than away from them. The places where an army could cross easily would have been well known to the local ruler, and it would have been a logical move to await an invader on your own side of the river as he struggled to reform his troops after the crossing.

The actual bank of a watercourse would not, however, normally have been a suitable spot for a battle. Before they were deepened and straightened for navigation and drainage purposes, the courses of rivers and streams were less well defined than they are today, with numerous small meanders and extensive marshy floodplains spreading into the countryside on either bank, and it must have been very difficult to find firm ground there on which to deploy. Other factors would also deter a defender from simply lining up his men along a river bank. Such a locality would be uncomfortable and unhealthy in wet weather, and might even be dangerous if sudden flooding was a possibility. And an invader whose passage was blocked in this way would probably not try to force his way across, but would instead leave a detachment behind to pin the defenders in place while he found an uncontested crossing up or downstream, which would automatically place him on the flank of the defenders and force them to withdraw.

At Maldon in 991 Ealdorman Byrhtnoth is said to have deliberately pulled back and allowed the Vikings to cross the River Blackwater, as the only way of bringing them to battle. Furthermore, an enemy who was allowed to cross and then obliged to fight with his back to the river would find it very difficult to retreat if he was defeated, as happened to Penda at the Winwaed in 654. For all these reasons, battles described as being fought on rivers are likely to have taken place not at the crossings themselves, but on the slightly higher ground beyond.

Waterways can of course be arteries of communication as well as obstacles, but there is little evidence for their use as such in this period. Even the Vikings travelled across the country mainly on stolen horses. In central England only the Rivers Severn, Trent and Thames were large and reliable enough to be viable military routes. In Offa's reign the monastery at Breedon-on-the-Hill near Burton on Trent was charged with providing hospitality for 'envoys from across the sea', which suggests that the main route into Mercia for foreign diplomats and traders was via the Humber estuary and the River Trent, which flows some five miles north of Breedon. On the other hand Nennius refers to two main rivers of Britain, the

Thames and the Severn, 'on which ships once travelled', implying that they no longer did so in his day, and perhaps had never done on other rivers. Many smaller streams which might otherwise have been adequate for navigation were obstructed by fish weirs. These were apparently an Anglo-Saxon invention, which consisted of lines of wooden traps placed across the current to catch migrating fish. Rackham describes these devices as being placed between an island and one bank, leaving the other side of the island open, but there is evidence that in places they proliferated to the extent that they became a hindrance to shipping and even obstructed the flow of water. In the eleventh century Edward the Confessor had to order the destruction of many of these weirs, which were blocking rivers as big as the Thames, Severn, Trent and Yorkshire Ouse.

Another factor which tended to force military operations to follow certain routes was the existence of a road network. As discussed below (page 29) the Roman transport system had by no means disappeared, and most of their major roads remained in use. There was also an extensive network of smaller local roads, and nearly one in eight of the features mentioned in the charters is a road or path (Rackham). Many of these are referred to as a 'herepath', or 'army path'. Rackham, however, considers that the identifiable 'army paths' do not constitute a deliberately planned strategic road system, and are unlikely to have been constructed specifically for military movements. It is noteworthy that although labour services were required by the Mercian kings from at least the eighth century for the purposes of building and repairing bridges and fortifications, road work was not included in these obligations, although local communities may have been expected to maintain the routes through their own neighbourhoods. Probably the term 'herepath' merely indicates a through route wide enough to be used by an army – or which had been used by one within living memory – in contrast to a lane used only by local people. It is worth remembering in this context that in the laws of King Ine, laid down in early eighth-century Wessex, a 'here' meant any armed force of thirty-five men or more.

19

Other place name evidence suggests that, after the Romans left, many of their bridges were initially neglected – the common name Stratford implies a ford on a Roman street, at a place where there would originally have been a bridge – but that Anglo-Saxon rulers were soon repairing them and ordering the construction of new ones. In Mercia King Aethelbald appears to have introduced an obligation on landowners in 749 to supply labour for work on bridges as well as fortresses. A sixth of the river crossings mentioned in charters between the seventh and tenth centuries were bridges, many of which crossed substantial water features. At Fambridge in Essex the River Crouch is a quarter of a mile wide, and although no bridge survives today, the name clearly implies its former existence (Rackham). A wooden causeway across the Thames marshes at Oxford has been dated to the reigns of Offa or his successor Coenwulf, and tree ring evidence has produced a date for the bridge at Cromwell, on the Trent near Newark, of between 740 and 750 (Brooks).

Chapter 2

The People of the Frontier

The Mercians first appear as a distinct group in the accounts of
Bede and the Anglo-Saxon Chronicle relating to the early seventh
century. By then they were already a long-established people, with
some of their oral traditions – such as the genealogies of their kings
– going back several hundred years. Attempting to trace their
origins, however, takes us into the most obscure and controversial
period in the whole of English history. According to the conventional view the 'English' people were easily distinguished by their
Germanic language and culture from the 'Celtic' or 'British' occupants
of northern and western Britain, and this difference is said to have
originated with the mass migrations of Anglo-Saxon tribes from
the Continent after the fall of the Roman Empire. Until the 1970s
it was generally accepted that the present inhabitants of most of
England were descended from these migrants, who had displaced
the aboriginal Britons with various degrees of force. Since then a
growing revisionist movement has cast doubt on this view, with
estimates of the size of the immigrant contribution declining to the
point where many archaeologists now deny that there is any
evidence for an Anglo-Saxon migration at all, preferring to think in
terms of imported fashions and cultural influences rather than
people (Pryor, 2004).

In the past the waters have been further muddied by politically
motivated ideas of history. Eighteenth- and nineteenth-century
English scholars often shared the prevailing contempt for the
peoples of the 'Celtic fringe' and wished to emphasise the distinct-

21

ness of the English and their supposedly superior political institutions, while more recently Celtic nationalists have also found it convenient to accentuate the same differences. Even today opinions tend to be so polarised that it is worth pointing out that the extreme migrationist view originates not from some Victorian ideologue, but from no less an authority than the Venerable Bede.

Bede's account of the coming of the English begins with the troubles which afflicted the Britons after the departure of the Roman armies early in the fifth century AD. The inhabitants of the former Roman province, now mostly converted to Christianity, are described as timid and demoralised, hiding in terror behind their fortifications while the barbarian Picts and Irish plundered the country. In the 440s they wrote to the Roman consul Aetius in Gaul, begging for help: 'The barbarians drive us into the sea, and the sea drives us back to the barbarians. Between these, two deadly alternatives confront us, drowning or slaughter.' But Aetius was already fully occupied with the war against Attila and his Huns, and no help could be sent. Meanwhile the Britons had rallied and temporarily driven off the invaders, but famine, followed by a terrible plague, caused many deaths and weakened them still further. Fearing that their enemies would soon return, they followed the advice of one of their kings, Vortigern, and hired German-speaking Saxon mercenaries from the Continent to defend them.

This, says Bede, happened during the reign of the Roman emperor Martianus, who came to the throne in the year 449. Vortigern brought over three shiploads of Saxon warriors, and they were given land in the eastern part of the country in return for military service. They quickly proved their worth by defeating a Pictish invasion from the north, then sent back to Saxony for more recruits, adding, in Bede's words, 'that the country was fertile and the Britons cowardly'. This sparked off a land rush which brought immigrants from the territories of three of the most warlike pagan tribes of Germany – the Saxons, the Angles and the Jutes. Soon they were settling in such numbers that the Britons became afraid. Bede does not specifically say that the Germans brought their families with them, but it is clear that he regarded this as a large-scale

22

settlement of peoples rather than just a collection of pillaging war bands. He goes on to state that the various English peoples of his day were all descended from these newcomers: the occupants of Kent, and the Isle of Wight and the mainland opposite, from the Jutes; those of Essex, Sussex and Wessex from the Saxons; and the East and Middle Angles, the Northumbrians, the Mercians and 'other English peoples' from the Angles.

It was the latter who precipitated the catastrophe which was to overwhelm the native Britons, when they made an alliance with the Picts and attempted to extort more land and provisions from their British employers. Whether or not they were successful in this we are not told, but eventually they broke out of the enclave where they had settled and began to ravage the country 'from the eastern to the western shores'. There was no organised opposition and the Anglian war bands inflicted terrible damage, destroying buildings, murdering bishops and priests as well as laymen and forcing the survivors to flee overseas or take refuge in the hills. Bede's language implies a deliberate genocide: 'A few wretched survivors captured in the hills were butchered wholesale, and others, desperate with hunger, came out and surrendered to the enemy for food, although they were doomed to lifelong slavery even if they escaped instant massacre.'

After this devastating raid the invaders returned to their settlements, and the surviving Britons gradually rallied. Under the leadership of Ambrosius Aurelianus, said to have been the sole surviving man of 'Roman race' in the country, they inflicted a defeat on their enemies and a long struggle ensued, with neither side gaining a decisive advantage over the other. Eventually the Britons won a victory at the Battle of Mount Badon, which earned them peace for a generation. According to Bede this took place 'about forty four years' after the Anglo-Saxon invasions, which would place it around the year 500. This was not the end of the story, for both Bede and the Anglo-Saxon Chronicle record further campaigns as late as the early seventh century which are usually supposed to be part of a gradual westward expansion of the invaders at the expense of the Britons. In 552, for example, the West Saxon king Cynric routed a British

23

army at 'Searo byrig' (Old Sarum, outside Salisbury). In 577 his successors Cuthwine and Ceawlin defeated and killed three British kings at Dyrham in Somerset, and subsequently captured the towns of Gloucester, Cirencester and Bath. Then in 605 Aethelfrith of Northumbria killed 'a countless number of Welsh' at Chester, including Christian priests who had come to pray for a British victory.

Bede's account is not the only source for the Anglo-Saxon invasion. We also have the testimony of the British monk Gildas, who was writing much closer in time to the events he described, and who may have been the source of some of Bede's information. Gildas' book, evocatively entitled *On the Ruin of Britain* and written in Latin around 550, describes Vortigern's invitation to the Saxons, their arrival in three ships, later reinforced by 'a larger company', and their demands for extra provisions, followed by a brutal attack. However, Gildas' perspective was much narrower than Bede's. His main purpose was to depict the sufferings of his people as God's punishment for their sins and those of their rulers, and he mentions contemporary kings by name only to condemn them for their immorality. Most of the identifiable places he refers to are in the far south-west of what is now England, and the only invaders he discusses are the Saxons. The Anglo-Saxon Chronicle describes a series of campaigns against the 'Britons' or 'Welsh' which seem to be the same as the events related from the other side by Gildas, but again they give us only part of the picture, concentrating on the activities of Saxon pirates in Kent, Sussex and the region around the Solent. What is more, the Chronicle in its present form was not written down until the ninth century, and so it cannot necessarily be regarded as an independent authority for the events of 400 years before.

On Bede's evidence it was the Angles, the ancestors of the Mercians, who eventually conquered and occupied most of England north of the Thames after the temporary setback at Mount Badon. But we have no account of any military operations by which this extensive conquest might have been achieved. In the Anglo-Saxon Chronicle the Angles appear as if from nowhere. The earliest mention here of them as invaders appears in a poem about the Battle of

Brunanburgh inserted in the Chronicle under the year 937, which boasts that there had never been a greater slaughter, 'as books tell us ... since Angles and Saxons came here from the east, sought out Britain over the broad ocean ... overcame the Welsh, seized the country.' A passage of this date cannot be regarded as independent of Bede, though, especially in view of the specific appeal to the authority of 'books'.

The earliest mention of Angles in Britain, in fact, comes from a brief survey of the island in the *De Bello Gotthico* of Procopius of Caesarea (Stenton), who was writing only a decade or so after Gildas. According to Procopius, Britain was inhabited by three races: the native Britons, the 'Frissones' or Frisians, and the 'Angiloi'. But he says nothing of a recent invasion or migration. On the contrary, basing his account on the statements of some Angles who had accompanied a Frankish embassy to Constantinople, he states that the country and its people were so fertile that their surplus population regularly emigrated to the European mainland, where the Frankish king settled them in sparsely inhabited parts of his territory.

The presence of large numbers of Frisians in England is otherwise undocumented, but is not particularly surprising. They travelled widely as merchants and seaborne raiders, and the English language is remarkably similar to the Frisian dialects still spoken on the other side of the North Sea, in the coastal regions of what is now the Netherlands. It is possible that Procopius' Anglian informants used the term 'Frissones' to denote their Saxon neighbours, although such usage is not attested in England itself. But Sir Frank Stenton has pointed out that German traditions also describe a population movement from England around the sixth century, and that according to one version, recorded at Fulda in the ninth century, the Saxons of Germany were descended from 'Angli' who had come from Britain.

With our earliest sources in such a state of confusion it is tempting to sidestep the issue of ethnic identity, and in common parlance the term 'Anglo-Saxon' (which was already in use in late Anglo-Saxon times) is widely used to include the descendants of Angles, Saxons

25

and Jutes, as well as the smaller groups of Frisian and Frankish immigrants whom Bede also mentions. The Welsh writers were lumping them all together as 'Saxons' as early as the time of Nennius, around 800, while at the same time the word 'Welsh', derived from Old English 'wealh' or 'foreign', became attached to the Celtic-speakers of southern Britain.

There is plenty of evidence that the 'English' peoples all spoke mutually intelligible languages and considered themselves to belong to a common cultural tradition. For example, all the English royal houses except that of Essex claimed descent from the legendary hero (or god) Woden, who is identical to the Scandinavian Odin. However, the dialects of English written in the 'Anglian' regions from the seventh century onwards are readily distinguishable from those of the 'Saxons', and the differences were presumably more marked in earlier times. It therefore makes sense to see the Angles as somehow self-consciously different from the Saxons, Jutes and others, though as we shall see this was not necessarily due to their origin in a different location on the Continent.

So, according to the traditional view, the Mercians and their neighbours were descended from invaders from the Anglian homeland in Europe, which is usually located in what is now the Schleswig-Holstein region at the southern end of the Jutland Peninsula. These Angles took advantage of the weakness of the Britons after the Roman withdrawal to carry out a violent policy of 'ethnic cleansing', and then occupied the fertile lands vacated by their victims. They presumably penetrated inland via the rivers which flow into the Wash and the Humber estuary, and over a period of a century and a half, between about AD 450 and 600, pushed their settlement frontier west as far as the watershed between the east-flowing River Trent and the Severn, which runs south-westwards into the Bristol Channel. The name Mercian, which derives from the word 'mierce', meaning mark or frontier, suggests that this group formed the spearhead of the advance, gaining as a reward the rich farmlands of the Middle Trent Valley – the location of their heartland in historic times. This scenario could certainly explain the appearance in the centre of previously Celtic England

26

of a warlike people speaking a Germanic language, worshipping Germanic gods, and bringing with them many of the trappings of German military and civilian culture. However, on examination it presents more problems than it solves.

The first is an obvious point which has nevertheless eluded many with an emotional attachment to the Anglo-Saxons, from Bede to the present day. The numerous small groups which the document known as the Tribal Hidage (see below, page 39) reveals in central England in the seventh century, some of them comprising only a few hundred fighting men, can hardly represent the successors of an army of conquest. Even in the time of Penda in the 630s and 640s, the Mercians, who were eventually forged into a kingdom under his leadership, were just one tribe among many, their name so obscure that to their contemporaries their ruler was just 'King Penda', or 'Penda the Southumbrian' (in other words, from south of the River Humber), as though he were a mere warlord without a proper kingdom. There is no surviving tradition of battles fought against the Britons along the Trent, no source mentions an earlier Anglian conqueror, no later Mercian king harks back to one – at least not in England – and we find no trace of a powerful kingdom which might have recently fragmented into those two dozen or more little tribes.

Bede's allegation that 'the Angles' made a treaty with the Picts does imply some sort of central command, but even if true it refers to a very early stage in the invasion, when their force may have consisted of only a few ships' crews. The strong impression is that large-scale political organisation was new to the region in the middle of the seventh century. But only an organised military force could have driven a well-established native population from an area of this size. In more recent times independent groups of settlers without military organisation have displaced other peoples – in North America, South Africa and Australia, for example – but only with huge advantages in numbers and technology, and even then the process has never been quick or easy. In fact it has often been observed that no settlement frontier ever managed a sustained advance against an intact Native American society which had not already been disrupted by disease or military operations. The theory

27

that sixth-century Anglian farmers could have achieved such a result without greatly superior weapons or implausibly large numbers must depend solely on assertions of racial superiority over Bede's 'cowardly Britons'. In historic times the British kingdoms were themselves well organised, though, and furthermore were capable of launching fast mounted raids over long distances, as the famous epic poem *Y Gododdin* relates. Small groups of Anglo-Saxon settlers pushing ahead of the frontier would have been extremely vulnerable to such attacks. For a roughly comparable situation we can look to nineteenth-century Texas, where, even with the benefit of firearms, white settlers were unable to hold their ground against mounted Comanche raiders, let alone advance onto the plains without the support of the army.

Archaeology also casts doubt on Bede's story. The process he describes – the Britons abandoning their land and setting up refugee communities in the hills, widespread starvation due to the disruption of agriculture, and four decades of fighting across a deserted no man's land – should have left traces in the archaeological record. If fields are left unworked even for a couple of seasons in the English climate, they will become overgrown with grass and weeds and will require considerable effort to bring them back into cultivation. In five to ten years trees will start to spring up, and after forty years they will have reverted to forest. If these changes occur over a large area, they will affect the composition of the pollen which is found in large quantities in soil samples. Pollen analysis is now so sophisticated that archaeologists would expect to be able to detect a catastrophic change of population by sudden changes in the type of vegetation it indicates. No such changes have been found. Most analyses of field patterns also suggest continuity between the farmers of the Roman period and those of Anglo-Saxon England.

In the territories associated with the peoples known as the Stoppingas and Aro Saetna in what is now Warwickshire, Della Hooke (1985) has traced a pattern of tracks and drove roads running between the low-lying arable lands in the south-east and the wooded and hilly north-west, and has argued that these represent a survival into Anglo-Saxon times of pre-Roman stock-raising practices. Cattle and other animals could be driven regularly from one region to the other in order to take advantage of the grazing in these different environments at different times of the year. It is surely incredible that recent immigrants could have worked out such complex arrangements in a short time in an unfamiliar country, or that they would have so closely paralleled those of the previous inhabitants. The obvious conclusion is that the Stoppingas and the Aro Saetna had already been living in Warwickshire for a very long time, and the same is no doubt true of the rest of the tribes of what was to become Mercia.

A perhaps even more persuasive argument for continuity comes from the survival of Roman roads into the medieval and modern periods. As Rackham has pointed out, before the invention of tarmac, a road abandoned for even a few years would have provided an ideal habitat for thorn bushes, so that if people subsequently wished to reopen the route they would find it easier to make a new road rather than clear the old one. Roads which still follow the straight Roman routes must therefore have been in use more or less continuously, which implies continuous occupation of the places which they connect. Taking Essex as an example, Rackham observes that: 'Every few years, through the darkest of the Dark Ages, there has been somebody from Duddenhoe End and Brent Pelham to take a billhook to the blackthorn on two short stretches of Roman road.'

Another piece of admittedly negative evidence is the absence of the mass graves which might be expected if a population numbering hundreds of thousands had been massacred, or wiped out by plague or famine, over a short period. Some interesting work by a team led by Paul Budd on skeletons recovered from a fifth- or early sixth-century cemetery at West Heslerton in Yorkshire tends to support the above conclusions (Pryor, 2004). From its date and location it was thought likely that the cemetery would contain the remains of first-generation Anglian immigrants to Britain, and so they were subjected to a technique known as stable-isotope analysis, which uses trace elements in the teeth to determine where their owners spent their formative years. The results were surprising. Of twenty-four bodies tested, ten were of people who had grown up locally and another ten were from the west coast, on the far side of the Pennine Hills. This suggests that at the very least there had been no rigid east–west divide at that time between 'Angles' on one side of the watershed and 'Britons' on the other. The remaining four skeletons were identified as coming from Scandinavia, a region which might include the area where the Angles are supposed to have originated. Unfortunately for the migration theory, however, these people do not represent a band of conquerors. They were all women, and they had been buried with almost none of the grave goods that are traditionally associated with Anglo-Saxons, implying that they were not from the families of wealthy or powerful war leaders. So even if there were invasions from across the North Sea in this period, there were other movements that were apparently peaceful. The women could of course have been slaves captured in warfare, but if native Britons in Anglian Northumbria were owning Scandinavian slaves, the ethnic situation must still have been far more complex than traditional theories allow.

The advent of sophisticated genetic studies in the last few years promises eventually to solve the question of Mercian origins once and for all. Unfortunately the work published to date has generated some widely varying conclusions, leading even some of the most perceptive writers to dismiss the entire subject. In 2002 Michael Weale and colleagues tested the DNA of people living in seven small towns across England and Wales on a line running from Norfolk to Anglesey, the idea being that the populations of such places were likely to have remained broadly in the same locality since the 'migration' period. They found a dramatic difference between the English and Welsh results, and concluded that the population of England had been almost entirely replaced by immigrants from the Continent in a process that must have involved prolonged violence.

Professor Stephen Oppenheimer at Oxford University has argued that this study tells us nothing about when this replacement might have happened, that peaceful contacts across the North Sea over a much longer time period could have produced an indistinguishable outcome, and that the sample was, in any case, too small to be valid. He has employed a different approach which seems to produce

30

some more plausible results. By looking for exact DNA matches on specific chromosomes between England and the supposed Anglo-Saxon homelands, he estimates that immigration from these regions in the entire post-Roman period has amounted to about 5.5 per cent of the total male population, with up to 15 per cent in some areas of East Anglia and around the Wash, and correspondingly lower rates elsewhere (Oppenheimer). These figures represent an upper limit, as they may include many migrants from later centuries and make no allowance for greater population growth among the new arrivals once they settled in England, which might be expected if they represented a social elite. Using an estimate of one million for the total population, half of whom were males, this might represent a migration by up to 25,000 men altogether, of whom a large proportion would have travelled no further west than Norfolk or Lincolnshire. This would have been a very large army by early medieval standards, but even supposing that it is all accounted for by fifth- and sixth-century Angles, they could have arrived over several generations.

Hines (in Hawkes), arguing from the evidence of Continental warrior burials, states that Germanic armies of the time are unlikely to have consisted of more than a few hundred men. Most of the later arrivals may of course have been farmers rather than warriors, and have settled peacefully on land acquired by their friends or relatives. Living alongside them, on terms of wary coexistence if not actual friendship, would have been the original British population, not as Bede's wretched survivors, but constituting a large majority. A good analogy might be with the ninth- and tenth-century Danish settlement of the same areas, which replaced some of the local rulers and introduced new names for some of the villages, but left the existing inhabitants largely intact. In that case we should see the Mercians not as invaders, but as descendants of the Coritani, Cornovii, Dobunni and other tribes of Roman Britain, ruled by a foreign dynasty perhaps, and having adopted much of the foreigners' culture, but still essentially British.

This does not mean that there were no Germanic invaders at all, and Bede could hardly have expected to be taken seriously if he had invented the migration theory from scratch. It was, after all, supposed to have happened at a time which would have been within the limits of oral tradition when he was writing. However, modern genealogical experience has shown that families tend to remember ancestors who are unusual in some way, and by the eighth century a majority of the inhabitants of Mercia may well have believed, rightly, that they were descended from invaders from across the sea, even though in most cases they would be recalling one distant ancestor among many others who were locally born.

This relatively peaceful view of the Anglo-Saxon 'conquest' is still controversial, however, and several arguments can be mustered against it. We may legitimately wonder why the urban civilisation introduced by the Romans disappeared so completely – far more completely than it did across the Channel in France – if there had not been a mass influx of 'barbarians' into Britain. The answer seems to be that, as modern research is making increasingly apparent, Britain had never been very thoroughly Romanised in the first place. It was always a rather remote frontier province of the Empire, only superficially urbanised and with an economy that was heavily reliant on the presence of the army. When the legions left at the beginning of the fifth century, the stimulus which government spending had provided to trade and industry disappeared. At the same time the disturbances on the Continent interrupted communications with the Mediterranean, Roman coins ceased to circulate and the people abandoned the towns and rich villas which had now lost their reason for existence and were too expensive to maintain. Classic Roman civilisation was already losing ground in the fourth century, long before the supposed Germanic invasions, and it is unlikely that many people, apart from a very small Romanised elite, were sorry to see it go.

To later Christian writers the Roman Empire had become synonymous with the Catholic Church, and it was axiomatic that it must have been a good thing. Bede, for example, cites the letter to the consul Aetius as evidence that the people were eager for the Romans to return. But other writers contradict this claim. Nennius actually states that the Britons rose up and drove the Romans out, and Gildas in his polemic criticises them for their habit of rebelling, 'sometimes against God ... and often against foreign kings'. The Roman writer Zosimus appears to confirm this view when he states that barbarian invasions encouraged some of the inhabitants of the island to 'leave Roman control and live their own lives, free of Roman laws.' Roman laws may well have seemed oppressive, especially those which restricted people to hereditary occupations and prohibited civilians from bearing arms. In addition the burden of taxation under the later Empire fell disproportionately on the poor, while a small minority became fabulously rich. Salvian, in his *De Gubernatione Dei*, wondered that the ordinary subjects of the Empire did not desert en masse to the barbarians, observing cynically that 'the enemy is more merciful to them than the tax collectors.'

Similar factors may even explain the paradox that Christianity, which had become the official religion of the Empire under the emperor Theodosius in the late fourth century, continued to thrive in the west of Britain – the region where Roman influence had always been weakest – while apparently disappearing in the more Romanised east. Nevertheless, there is reason to believe that it had never been popular with ordinary Britons living under Roman rule, and it may have been discarded along with the rest of the discredited Roman way of life (Russell and Laycock). We also have the testimony of Bede that as late as the seventh century recently Christianised Anglo-Saxon kingdoms were apt to revert to their more familiar old pagan practices when under stress, as happened in Sussex during the plague of 664. In what were to become Wales and Cornwall, however, the new religion was less tarnished by association with the Roman occupation, and so it was able to spread further west to Ireland, and thence north to the Picts and Scots, on its own merits.

Another objection to the idea of ethnic continuity cites the presence of the English language, which is clearly related to Germanic dialects and just as clearly different from Welsh and other 'Celtic' tongues spoken in the west of the island. The usual explanation for this situation is that before the arrival of the Anglo-Saxons the whole of Britain was occupied by people speaking Celtic languages, but this is difficult to prove, as evidence for any native language in eastern Britain in Roman times is almost non-existent (Oppenheimer). People can replace their languages with new ones over time, as can be seen in Turkey and Hungary, for example, where Asiatic languages introduced by small numbers of conquerors from further east have replaced those originally spoken in historic times. It may be that English took over from whatever had preceded it much more slowly than our sources suggest; the documents we have are written in Latin or Old English, the languages of the ruling and literate classes, but there is little evidence of what the ordinary people were speaking until after the Norman Conquest. Alternatively, contacts across the North Sea between eastern England and northern Germany had probably been strong since the Iron Age, and Germanic language and culture may already have been established in the island, or at least have been familiar enough to facilitate their rapid adoption when Roman influence disappeared.

The extent of the economic decline of post-Roman Britain can be exaggerated, and despite the lack of archaeological evidence it is hard to believe that people forgot how to make pots, for example, or ceased to be able to carry out repair work on Roman buildings (Fleming). One reason for the apparent abandonment of Roman towns might have been eminently practical. Hydatius confirms some of Gildas' apocalyptic account when he says that a plague devastated 'almost the whole world' in the 440s, and although it has been argued that this is too late to be responsible for the situation in Britain it need not have been unique. Remains of the black rat, alleged to be the carrier of the bubonic plague of the Middle Ages, have been found in fifth-century deposits, and black rats are mainly creatures of towns and sea ports. Professor William McNeill has argued that Mediterranean civilisation was experiencing a prolonged period of stress from the second century AD onwards as a result of new diseases brought in via trade contacts with Asia, and it is not unlikely that people in Britain understood that their afflictions were somehow connected with Rome and its works.

One further obstacle to the idea of continuity between Britons and Anglo-Saxons needs to be addressed. Why would the devoutly

Christian Bede make up or promote a story which depicts his own ancestors as mass murderers who dispossessed the rightful owners of the country by force and treachery? The answer no doubt lies in his explicit view of the English as 'God's chosen people' by analogy with the Israelites of the Old Testament. His main grievance against the British of his own day was a theological one, deriving from the split between the Roman and Celtic churches over such matters as the authority of the Pope and the calculation of the date of Easter. Such matters were taken very seriously in the eighth century, when the conversion of the English was still a recent event, and the hold of the Catholic Church must still have seemed precarious. There seems also to have been a longstanding grievance over the allegation that the British churches had never tried to convert their neighbours, who had had to languish in heathen superstition until a mission arrived from Rome at the end of the sixth century. Bede was therefore predisposed to regard the Britons who followed the Celtic tradition as immoral, cowardly and lazy – especially as he was aware of the work of Gildas, who had said as much about his own people. It was therefore logical to identify the Britons with the Canaanites, whose violent dispossession by the Israelites on God's orders is described in the Book of Joshua. There was no reason to question Gildas' lurid account of the massacres perpetrated by the invaders of England, and since the conquest must have been God's will, the use of force tended to reinforce rather than undermine its legitimacy.

Chapter 3

Kingdoms and Armies

Whatever really happened during the sparsely documented fifth and sixth centuries, it is generally agreed that by the beginning of the seventh the process which would lead to the growth of the first true English kingdoms was well under way. We seem to be able to detect traces of a period in which the country was divided among a large number of small tribes, the results either of invasions or of local movements for autonomy after the end of Roman authority, which had gradually coalesced into larger political units. West of the Mercian heartland along the River Trent, for example, two once-independent peoples, the Magonsaetan and the Hwicce, retained their own rulers but were coming under increasing Mercian influence, culminating in the eighth century with the downgrading of their kings to 'subreguli', 'sub-kings', and eventually 'ealdormen' or 'earls', recognised to be of noble blood but no longer royal even in their own estimation.

If we assume that every group which is identified by a distinctive name had been independent in the immediately post-Roman decades, we can envisage the sixth century as a time of incessant small-scale warfare reminiscent of the 'Warring States' era of ancient China, in which the strongest prospered at the expense of their neighbours, emerging eventually from the spiral of violence as newly fledged kingdoms. In fact there is little evidence that this century was any more warlike than the ones which succeeded it, and most of the kingdoms may have come into being by intermarriage between closely related neighbours, whether 'British' or 'Anglo-Saxon', and other essentially peaceful processes. Edward James has suggested that the English kings may have extended their power in a similar fashion to Clovis, ruler of the Franks on the Continent in the late fifth century. According to his biographer Gregory of Tours, Clovis employed various devious means in preference to naked force, using Roman-style law codes and (after his conversion to Christianity) calling church councils to confer their reflected authority on him. He also systematically hunted down and assassinated other claimants to royal status, including his own relatives, and would express feigned astonishment at the ease with which their leaderless tribes and kingdoms fell into his hands, publicly attributing his success to divine favour (E. James, in Bassett).

From about 600 onwards, however, we start to see the English kingdoms fighting significant wars among themselves. It is sometimes argued that there was a significant ritual element in Anglo-Saxon warfare, with armies travelling by customary routes and meeting by mutual arrangement at some well-known landmark. In the seventh and eighth centuries each kingdom seems to have fought a major battle about once every twenty years, or once in a generation (Halsall, in Hawkes). This might reflect the requirement for a newly enthroned king to seek validation of his rule by success in war, or for a new generation of warriors to obtain glory and plunder. The 'hazelled field', 'holmganga' and other forms of formalised combat described in Scandinavian sources are often mentioned in support of this thesis, but their relevance to conditions in England seems to have been assumed without convincing evidence (see, for example, Pollington; Underwood). If early Anglo-Saxon kings ever issued formal challenges to each other to meet in battle or single combat like the Viking heroes, we do not hear of it.

An alternative interpretation sees the motivation for most of the wars of our period as economic or dynastic, and recognises that averaging out the frequency of recorded battles obscures the existence of extended periods of violence which we would call major wars. Penda of Mercia, for example, fought battles on average about once every three years between 628 and 654. These were certainly large-scale engagements by the standards of the time, as nearly all of the armies which Penda defeated were commanded by kings, at least five of whom met their deaths in the process. This was warfare at an intensity seldom equalled until the campaigns of Napoleon, but then Penda was fighting to establish the independence of his new kingdom against several longer-established neighbouring powers.

Mercia was doomed by its geographical position to be a country won and maintained by the sword. Its location in the centre of the country often obliged it to fight on several fronts in rapid succession: against the Welsh to the west, the Northumbrians to the north, the East Angles in the east and the West Saxons in the south. At the same time its central location gave it the advantage of interior lines of communication of which an energetic leader could take advantage to pick off his enemies one by one. As a rich agricultural country it supplied large numbers of warriors, but, being isolated from the coastal ports and trade routes, it was relatively poor in terms of the means to reward and recruit those warriors. Salt works at Droitwich and lead mines in the Peak District were exploited in late Anglo-Saxon times, and a late ninth-century charter tells us that tolls on Droitwich salt 'had always belonged to the king.'

The excavation of rich warrior burials at Sarre in Kent has led to suggestions that in a few places trade routes may have been lucrative enough to justify the establishment of military camps to guard them and collect tolls (Brooks). But lead and salt probably contributed little to the coffers of the Mercian kings in comparison to the rich deposits of both lead and silver in the Mendip Hills of Somerset, which were securely under West Saxon control. Other valuable metals, such as Welsh gold and the tin for which Cornwall was famous, were also monopolised by Mercia's often hostile neighbours. The relative scarcity of coin finds has sometimes been used as evidence for Mercian poverty, and although the centre of the country is turning out to have been less of a backwater than was once thought, what metal detectors call 'productive sites' are probably still less common there than in the coastal regions where overseas trade was concentrated (Pryor, 2006). This explains the main strategic ambition of all the Mercian kings from the late seventh century onwards. Penda, fighting an essentially defensive war, looked mainly to the north, towards his most formidable enemy, Northumbria. His successors focused rather on the south-east, where London and the ports of Kent, with their connections across the English Channel, promised the means to enrich and develop the new kingdom.

Mercia and the Tribal Hidage

One of the most interesting and controversial documents in Anglo-Saxon history may provide us with a unique snapshot of the political situation in central England at the beginning of Penda's career. The 'Tribal Hidage' is preserved in seven later copies, which are generally agreed to derive from an original drawn up in the seventh or eighth centuries. However, scholars continue to argue over its exact date, origin and purpose. It takes the form of a list of political groupings, kingdoms or 'tribes' of varying sizes, with an assessment for each in numbers of 'hides'. In later law codes a hide was theoretically supposed to be 120 acres, or as much agricultural land as one plough team could cultivate in a year. In practice, though, it was a unit of value rather than acreage, equivalent to the territory needed to support a single family or fighting man. Although often reproduced, the Hidage is worth including here because of its likely importance for the military organisation of Mercia throughout our period. (The names are in, as near as possible, their original form using the modern English alphabet, but the assessments have been converted into numerals for ease of reference).

Myrcna landes	30,000 hides
Wocen saetna	7,000
Westerna	7,000
Pecsaetna	1,200
Elmed saetna	600
Lindesfarona with Haethfeldlande	7,000
Suth gyrwa	600
North gyrwa	600
East wixna	300

39

West wixna	600
Spalda	600
Wigesta	900
Herefinna	1,200
Sweord ora	300
Gifla	300
Hicca	300
Wiht gara	600
Noxgaga	5,000
Ohtgaga	2,000

At this point is inserted a total for the above (incorrect) of 66,100 hides.

Hwinca	7,000
Ciltern saetna	4,000
Hendrica	3,500
Unecung-ga	1,200
Arosaetna	600
Faerpinga	300
Bilmiga	600
Widerigga	600
Eastwilla	600
Westwilla	600
East engle	30,000
Eastsexena	7,000
Cantwarena	15,000
Suthsexena	7,000
Westsexena	100,000

The grand total of these entries, we are told, is 242,700 hides.

Whereas the identity of some of these groups is obvious, others are more obscure and some are known only from this single source. Some general principles are, however, immediately apparent. The Hidage does not cover the whole of England in similar detail. Most of Northumbria is missing, and the south and east (the East Angles, South, East and West Saxons, and the 'Cantwarena' or inhabitants of

40

Kent) are not analysed below the level of the main kingdoms. ('Lindesfarona', incidentally, refers to Lindsey, roughly corresponding to modern Lincolnshire, and not to Lindisfarne in Northumbria.) Central England, by contrast, is divided into about twenty-seven entities ranging in size from 'Myrcna landes', or Mercia proper, down to tiny groups of 300 hides, which would represent not much more than a cluster of villages. Of the bigger entities, the 'Hwinca' are presumably the Hwicce, who at this date still had their own ruling dynasty but were already subject to the Mercian kings, and the 'Westerna' are often identified with the similarly situated Magonsaetan, one of whose kings, Merewalh, was alleged to have been Penda's son (M. Gelling, in Bassett).

Two possible reasons for this uneven coverage are commonly put forward. One is that this is a Mercian document, probably of the eighth century, drawn up by clerks familiar with the internal subdivisions of their own kingdom, but not with those of their neighbours. On the other hand, if it was produced elsewhere it might reflect the actual condition of the area before the Mercian kings imposed their authority on it. This question cannot be settled from examination of the later surviving copies, but Brooks (in Bassett) argues that it is a tribute list, and that the most likely place of origin is Northumbria, precisely because the Northumbrian kingdoms of Bernicia and Deira do not appear – no king, after all, would impose tribute on himself. If this is correct, the Hidage must date from a period when a Northumbrian ruler claimed some sort of supremacy over the whole of southern England. Brooks favours Oswy's short-lived supremacy after the death of Penda in 654. The other obvious candidate is Edwin, whose career is discussed below, and who, according to the Anglo-Saxon Chronicle, conquered the whole of Britain except for Kent. The Cantwarena might have been included in the list more in hope than expectation, or they may have promised to pay the tribute in order to avoid a Northumbrian invasion.

Higham (1995) goes even further, suggesting that the list was completed in 626, in a brief period of triumph when Edwin seemed to have cowed even Wessex. It should be pointed out that others dispute

41

this theory, and even doubt that it is a tribute list at all, suggesting that it may have been created in eighth-century Mercia as a sort of primitive census or tax assessment. In favour of an early Northumbrian provenance, however, are the archaic look of many of the 'tribal' names, and the suspiciously arbitrary valuations in multiples of 300 or 1,000. It is not likely that these ever bore much relation to the real extent of the territories mentioned, or the resources of their populations. The huge assessment of 100,000 hides for Wessex, in particular, may be deliberately punitive, if not entirely wishful thinking. If the Hidage really is a picture of central England in the 620s it is of great interest for our story. It explains how neighbouring powers could march unmolested across what was later to become Mercian territory to pursue their feuds against each other, because at that time there was no central authority in most of the country. It also explains why the Anglo-Saxon Chronicle prefers to call Penda's people 'Southumbrians' rather than Mercians, because at that time the term 'Mercia' was still restricted to one kingdom among many.

'How the Folk-Kings Flourished' (*Beowulf*)

At the head of a kingdom, by definition, was a 'cyning' or king, and our earliest written sources take the institution of monarchy as given, describing people and places according to their allegiance to geographically based kings and kingdoms. However, it is not clear exactly what distinguished a king from any other aristocratic leader. A king required a military following, but possession of one did not automatically confer the title, as is shown by the Anglo-Saxon Chronicle's remark about the thirty commanders in Penda's army at the Winwaed, that 'some of them were kings'. The genealogies with which new rulers are routinely introduced in the same source show that royal blood was considered to be important, but these family trees are not very convincing to modern eyes, with their descent from legendary gods or heroes such as Woden. The Chronicle contents itself on occasion with an unsupported assertion that 'that kin goes to Cerdic', the semi-legendary founder of Wessex, while in Christian times it was sometimes thought advisable to take the line all the way back to Adam, as in the entry for the year 855 discussing

42

the ancestry of the West Saxon King Aethelwulf. The question therefore arises whether a man was eligible to become king because of his ancestry, or whether it was customary to concoct a suitable royal line of descent for whoever achieved that status. It is certain that there were no fixed rules regarding the succession, because the kings in the sources are very often not the sons but the brothers or cousins of their predecessors, or – especially in ninth-century Mercia – have no known relationship to them at all.

This led E.A. Freeman and other nineteenth-century writers to suppose that the Anglo-Saxon states were essentially democratic, their kings being elected from among the eligible candidates by the 'witan' or royal council. 'In every kingdom', Freeman argued, 'there was a royal family, out of which alone, under all ordinary circumstances, kings were chosen; but within that royal family the Witan of the land had a free choice.' This view has long since been discarded by scholars, not least because there is no evidence of any constitution, written or otherwise, which could have laid down such a rule. We also know that what we think of as 'feudal' hierarchies of loyalty and obligation already existed, and would have constrained the choice of anyone who was in a position to nominate a king. On the other hand rulers must in a sense have been 'chosen', because in the absence of a strict law of succession no one could obtain the throne without strong support within the kingdom. This helped if anything to strengthen the institution, because a candidate who was obviously unfit to rule would lack sufficient backing from the start.

We do not hear of long periods of weak government during royal minorities, as happened in the later Middle Ages; Coenred of Mercia, for example, did eventually succeed his father Wulfhere, but not until twenty-nine years after Wulfhere's death in 675. At that time he had apparently been an infant, so the throne had passed instead to his uncle Aethelred. On other occasions the situation was less clear cut, but even when it was necessary to fight for the throne this at least ensured that it passed to a successful warrior. Offa himself, we are told, though widely recognised as a worthy ruler, had had to fight a civil war against at least one rival and seize power 'through bloodshed'.

A king's primary role was as a leader of warriors, and like every Anglo-Saxon nobleman he based his power on his following of armed 'heorthgeneatas', or 'hearth companions'. Often referred to as 'gesiths', or from the eighth century onwards as 'thegns', these men were bound to him by personal ties of loyalty. The ideal at least is illustrated by the story in the Anglo-Saxon Chronicle of the killing of King Cynewulf of Wessex. The leader of the assassins, Cyneheard, tried to persuade the men who came to avenge the king to desert, pointing out that some of their relatives were serving with his forces: 'and then they said that no relative was dearer to them than their lord, and they would never follow his slayer.' The poem on the Battle of Maldon takes this view of loyalty to an extreme, describing how the retainers of Earl Byrhtnoth refused to flee from a lost battle against the Vikings, preferring to die to a man beside the body of their lord. They were rallied by a Mercian noble named Aelfwine, who reminded them of the boasts they had made when drinking their lord's mead in his hall, and ended with the challenge: 'Now whoever is brave may prove it.'

Needless to say this did not always happen in practice, as the history of Penda's wars shows: one king after another died in battle with his armies, and in each case their followers fled. On at least one occasion, at Maserfelth, their lord's body was left ignominiously on the field to be mutilated by the victors. As usual it was not the institution of the 'hearth companions' that mattered so much as the personal qualities of the men concerned, and a reference in *Beowulf* suggests that the 'hall fellow', a poser whose boasts in the mead hall were not backed up by action on the battlefield, was as well known in Anglo-Saxon England as in any other society.

As the head of a court and a military retinue which were essentially unproductive in economic terms, a king had to secure supplies of food and other necessary goods from the farming population of the territory under his control. There were four main ways of doing this, all of which had a bearing on military strategy. Firstly, a ruler could travel around his kingdom and live for a while as a guest of each local community or magnate, effectively consuming his tax revenue at source. This sort of 'royal progress' remained popular until the end of the Middle Ages, and it had the advantage of providing a king's subjects with direct access to him in return for their expenditure. However, it has been argued that even in the seventh century the economy of most of England, and the condition of its roads, were not so primitive as to make this necessary (Kirby). The widely separated localities from which charters were issued prove that kings did travel, on campaign and for other reasons, but they probably did not have to do so in search of subsistence. Instead there is already evidence for the existence of royal estates, often indicated by the place name suffix '-tun'; these served as local administrative centres and collection points for food rents, which could either be consumed on the estate or forwarded elsewhere. There is evidence that these estates were often fortified, and although at first they are unlikely to have consisted of more than a palisaded earth bank around a wooden hall, the history of the Mercian Wars shows that these could be of considerable strategic significance.

Outside the areas which were firmly under a king's control there might be a wide belt of territory in which his power was at least grudgingly recognised, and taxation (or rather tribute) was collected in the form of livestock, especially cattle, transported 'on the hoof' to the central regions. This, it has been argued, was seen as a humiliating relationship because those who contributed their cattle received nothing in return, except perhaps nominal protection from raiding. They would therefore be the first to break away if the king died or suffered a serious reverse on the battlefield. In fact the distinction between the collection of this tribute and a violent cattle raid was not always clear. A poem in praise of Cadwallon, the early seventh-century king of Gwynedd in North Wales, says that his cattle 'have not bellowed before the spear points' of King Edwin's Northumbrians, meaning that he has asserted his independence and not allowed them to be taken away (T. Charles-Edwards, in Bassett).

Finally, in the outermost zone surrounding the kingdom, were hostile but weaker states which could be simply raided, their possessions looted and their animals driven off. In a subsistence economy in which food supplies were always precarious, these beasts could themselves be an important strategic resource. Although our sources never describe it specifically, we can imagine a continuous one-way movement of cattle into Mercia from those neighbouring kingdoms which were at least temporarily forced to acknowledge the supremacy of its rulers. Then the beef, converted into human muscle by means of the feasting in the mead halls, would be re-exported in the armies of men such as Wulfhere, Aethelbald and Offa to preserve and extend their dominance.

The Warrior Class

Despite the assertions of nineteenth-century scholars that the early Anglo-Saxons were an egalitarian people in which every man was a warrior, it seems that military service in the seventh century was normally restricted to the noble class. The main distinction was institutionalised in several sets of surviving laws through the concept of the 'wergild' or 'man price'. By the late seventh century it was becoming common practice to regulate the old system of blood feuds by imposing fines on those who wrongly killed their fellows, instead of leaving the onus on the victims' families to avenge them. The laws of Ine of Wessex, who ruled from 688 to 726, are one of the earliest surviving statements of this principle. They divide society into two broad classes: the thegns or gesiths, whose wergild was set at 1,200 shillings, and the 'ceorls' or commoners, whose lives were worth only one-sixth as much. Foreigners, usually but not necessarily identified with the British, had a wergild half that of the equivalent Saxons.

In this context the story of Imma, as related by Bede, is especially illuminating. Imma was a Northumbrian thegn who was knocked unconscious at the Battle of the River Trent in 679, and on recovering found that his comrades had fled. He tried to escape, presumably discarding his weapons and armour in the process, but was captured by the Mercians. When they took him to their leader for interrogation he decided to conceal the fact that he was a warrior, afraid that he might be held for ransom or killed to avenge Mercian losses. Imma therefore pretended to be what Bede calls a 'rusticus', a peasant or ceorl, explaining his presence on the battlefield by saying that he had been transporting food for the supply train. However, his captors soon realised from his clothing, speech and general appearance that he was of noble birth, and he was persuaded to reveal the truth in exchange for a promise not to harm him. Imma was told that in that case that he deserved to die in revenge for the deaths of the Mercian leader's brothers and other relatives in the battle, but instead he was sold to a Frisian slave trader in London, and eventually ransomed by the intervention of King Hlothere of Kent.

Bede tells this tale as part of a typical miracle story, alleging that Imma's brother, who was a priest, had believed him to be dead and had said numerous masses for his soul. As a side effect Imma was released from earthly chains rather than spiritual ones, and whenever his captors tried to put him in fetters they miraculously fell off. The rest of the account, however, seems fairly plausible, and it tells us a great deal about the experience of warfare in the seventh century.

The presence on a battlefield of a man who was not a member of the professional warrior class clearly required explanation, so we can assume that if ordinary ceorls did fight, they were in a minority. Class differences were marked enough to doom Imma's deception to failure, and furthermore, although the two sides spoke a common language, his enemies could easily tell that he was not a Mercian. Perhaps the Northumbrian accent was noticeably different, or perhaps the armies were small enough for the leaders to know their own men by sight. It is unlikely that any sort of military uniform or field sign was involved, because Imma would hardly have attempted to claim non-combatant status if he had been wearing one. We also discover from this affair that even in wars between Christian kingdoms it was accepted practice to kill prisoners to expiate a blood feud, or to sell them into slavery. In addition there is evidence of a kind of international brotherhood among the nobility, despite the Mercians' unchivalrous behaviour towards their victim:

Hlothere's involvement came about because Imma had once been in the service of his aunt, the Northumbrian queen Etheldreda.

A conclusion which is increasingly finding favour is that most seventh- and eighth-century armies consisted entirely of professional or semi-professional warriors, the thegns belonging either directly to the king or to one of his noble vassals. Where Bede and the Anglo-Saxon Chronicle give specific dates for the campaigns and battles which they mention it is clear that they usually occurred between August and November – in other words, during the period between the gathering of the grain harvest and the onset of winter weather. This need not mean, however, that the men who fought these wars were not available earlier because they were personally involved in the harvesting. The need to collect supplies of bread to accompany the army, and the hope of seizing the enemy's grain without the labour of harvesting it oneself, would be sufficient to account for this timing.

Ine imposed fines for avoiding military service, depending on the rank of the offender. A gesith paid 120 shillings and forfeited his land if he held any; if he had no land he was fined half that amount. A ceorl had to pay thirty shillings. However, the code does not specifically state that all ceorls had to serve, or in what capacity. A man who could afford to pay thirty shillings would in any case have belonged to the wealthiest stratum of his class, and was probably obliged to fight as an exceptional condition of a particular grant of land. Armies would therefore have been predominantly aristocratic, with a much higher proportion of men carrying expensive swords and wearing armour than the occurrence of these items in the population as a whole would suggest. They might also have been all mounted on horseback and so highly mobile, although Imma's story shows that peasants would accompany large expeditions to transport supplies, presumably in carts, which must have slowed the army down. Small raiding parties would probably have been expected to live off the land.

What do we mean, though, by 'large' and 'small' in this context? How big were the armies which fought the Mercian Wars? Writers on this subject usually quote from Ine's laws, which defined any

48

armed force of over thirty-five men as a 'here' or raiding army. This does not of course mean that this was a typical size for armies, merely that it was considered too big to be dismissed as a mere band of robbers, and so perhaps required the attention of the king rather than being left to local leaders to deal with. It does suggest that the 'thousands' of casualties in the battle accounts of Henry of Huntingdon and others are wild exaggerations, but another of Henry's observations may receive unexpected support. He was aware of the paradox that many of the Anglo-Saxon battles which he describes lasted a whole day and involved heavy losses on both sides without leading to a decisive result, whereas the conflicts of his own day were usually over in a much shorter time. His explanation was that the warriors of an earlier age had been stronger, and possessed more stamina and courage, than their feeble descendants of the twelfth century, who were liable to run as soon as the fight turned against them. This sounds like a typical eulogy for the 'good old days' when 'men were men', but might have a basis in fact. Henry was writing at the time of the 'Anarchy' of King Stephen's reign, when England had been relatively peaceful for two generations, and its military caste may indeed have lacked the professionalism of the veterans who had fought in the relentless wars of Penda, Aethelbald and Offa. Perhaps in their time men such as Imma would have been instantly distinguishable from the peasantry not only by their equipment but by their stature and muscular development, the product of a high-protein diet and constant training. A similar situation exists even today in places such as parts of rural India, where the local subsistence farmers can be readily told apart from those who make their living in other – sometimes less legitimate – ways.

The professional gesiths of early Anglo-Saxon times may even have constituted a hereditary military class which operated across the borders of the developing kingdoms, as we have seen in the case of Imma. Bede also mentions that many young men from other kingdoms served in the retinue of King Oswine of Deira (reigned 644–51). On the other hand men of this caste seem often to have embarked on private freebooting expeditions at the expense of neighbouring kingdoms, especially perhaps the Britons. According to his biographer, an East Anglian monk named Felix, Saint Guthlac, who was born among the Middle Angles in the late seventh century, decided to follow the example of 'valiant heroes of old', and gathered a following of similar warlike youths whom he led on raids in search of wealth and glory. From another passage in the same source we learn that Guthlac had once lived among the Britons and spoke their language, so some of his military career had presumably been spent in Wales. After nine years as a war leader he renounced warfare and became a monk. Guthlac is only known to us because his later reputation for sanctity attracted the attention of the chroniclers, but many of his contemporaries no doubt used the experience and military knowledge which they had gained to enter the service of a king or nobleman as one of his hearth companions. For this reason their youthful escapades were tolerated for the skills and experience which they imparted to the future warriors, despite the risk of them provoking hostilities with neighbouring kingdoms.

At some point during the eighth century military obligations began to be placed on a more formal basis with the appearance of 'bookland'. This was land granted by the king in return for certain specific obligations set out in a 'book' or charter. It is of course likely that these obligations were based on those required in previous centuries, but which had not been written down. Professor Brooks, in a detailed survey of military obligations in the charters, concluded that this development began in Mercia during the reign of Aethelbald and spread gradually to neighbouring kingdoms under Mercian influence, reaching Kent during Offa's occupation in the 790s. What became the three 'common burdens' – service in the army, work on fortifications and work on building and maintaining bridges – are first specified in King Aethelbald's charter of 749 (Brooks). This monarch incurred the wrath of the church by attempting to impose military obligations on religious houses as well as secular landlords, but even Offa was insistent that there were no exemptions from these three forms of service. In fact it has been suggested that it was Offa who permanently extended his predecessor's labour dues to include military service. No doubt local lords discharged their obligations by compelling their own tenants to turn out for labouring or supply-train duties, but there is still little evidence that the mass of the people actually fought in the armies.

Still influential in Anglo-Saxon studies is Warren Hollister's theory that in the eleventh century the army was divided into two main elements, the 'great fyrd', or mass levy, and the 'select fyrd', an elite force consisting of one man selected from every five hides. This has often been extended by other writers to apply to the whole Anglo-Saxon period, but even for the period with which Hollister was concerned there are few references to this system in contemporary documents. In the era of the Mercian kings the term 'fyrd' was used, as in the Anglo-Saxon Chronicle, to describe a defensive force or levy, as opposed to a 'here' or raiding army. The Vikings were a 'here', but then so were the forces of Offa, Alfred and other English kings when operating beyond their own frontiers. It is reasonable to expect that the composition of a 'fyrd' would differ in some way from that of a 'here', but battle accounts shed little light on this. If defensive armies routinely included large numbers of locally recruited peasants their fighting power must have been minimal, because enemy 'raids' frequently defeated them. The situation seems to have changed at the end of the ninth century during the reign of Alfred, who introduced a system of rotating service, whereby half the army was in the field at any one time, the remainder working on the land or garrisoning fortifications (Abels). This was an emergency measure introduced to combat the Viking invasions, and must have required a more extensive call-up in order to keep the field forces up to a reasonable strength. It also implies that men whose usual occupation was agriculture were now being expected to fight for the first time.

The armies of the early Anglo-Saxon period, then, were relatively small in size and simple in structure, but commanding them must nevertheless have been more than a matter of swinging a sword in the front rank. Unfortunately we have little data on the details of command and control. Leaders were obviously expected to set an example: at Maldon the army fell into confusion when a coward stole the earl's horse to make his escape, and some men concluded that their commander had deserted them. Before the same battle Byrhtnoth is portrayed as riding along the ranks, exhorting the warriors to keep in formation and reminding the more nervous or inexperienced among them how to hold their shields firmly.

It is likely that a leader would be accompanied by some sort of standard to mark his position, and perhaps help in conveying simple orders such as a general advance or retreat. Bede says that Edwin of Northumbria had a royal standard of a type 'known to the Romans as a "tufa", and to the English as a "tuf"', and although he mentions this as proof of Edwin's exceptional status, Roman-inspired insignia may have been fairly common. The dragon-shaped 'windsock' standards shown on the Bayeux tapestry are very similar to the late Roman 'draco', which suggests that they had been in use since a very early date. King Cuthred of Wessex is said by Henry of Huntingdon to have had a standard bearing a golden dragon at the Battle of Beorhford in 752, and the 'dragon' associated with Alfred the Great was probably very similar, if it was not actually the same one. Henry's account also refers to a Mercian standard bearer, but unfortunately we have no specific descriptions of Mercian flags, although 'emblazoned standards shining with gold' are mentioned at the same battle. Representations on coins as well as the Bayeux tapestry suggest that flags at this date were triangular, and supported by a crosspiece at the top of the shaft as well as being attached to the shaft itself. Others may have been of the type known to the Romans as a 'vexillum', which was rectangular and attached only to a crosspiece along the top. Alternatively Christian kings could make use of tall processional crosses to motivate their men, especially in battles against pagan opponents, as suggested by Bede's accounts of the seventh-century Northumbrians at Denisesburn and Maserfelth, discussed below.

Chapter 4
Penda's Wars

From the beginning of the seventh century we start to discern a coherent picture of the political map of the British Isles. What is now Scotland was divided among three more or less distinct peoples: the Picts, the original inhabitants of the country north of the narrow neck formed by the Forth and Clyde estuaries; the Scots of the south-western Highlands, ruled by a dynasty of Irish origin; and the Britons of Strathclyde in the far south-west, who were related by language and culture to the Welsh. Most of what is now the northern half of Wales was ruled by the kings of Gwynedd, who controlled Anglesey, Snowdonia and the north coast, and Powys, further south and east along the border with what is now Shropshire.

These two kingdoms were the principal enemies of Mercia in Offa's day, and may once have controlled territory as far west as the Middle Severn Valley, whose loss to the emerging kingdom of Mercia, probably towards the end of the sixth century, was a continuing source of grievance to them. Possibly the Magonsaetan and the Hwicce had once been vassals of Gwynedd or Powys, and their defection to Mercia had led to the establishment of the historical frontier between England and Wales. Gwent and Dyfed, in South Wales, were more often at war with Wessex, the kingdom of the West Saxons, who appear to have driven the Welsh out of Somerset and Gloucestershire during the late sixth century. England was divided among the kingdoms of what we know, following Henry of Huntingdon, as the 'Heptarchy', consisting of the seven kingdoms of Kent, East Anglia, Northumbria, Mercia, and the East, South and

53

West Saxons. This is in fact a simplified view, as several of these kingdoms – including Mercia – were evidently still in the process of consolidation from the chaos of petty tribes and chiefdoms from which they are believed to have originated. Northumbria in particular was a very recent creation at this time, formed from the older kingdoms of Bernicia and Deira.

In his chapter relating the conversion of King Edwin of Northumbria in 627, Bede refers in passing to the mother of two of Edwin's sons, a certain 'Coenburg, daughter of Cearl, King of the Mercians'. He adds that these children were born while Edwin was in exile, presumably in Mercia, during the reign of his predecessor Aethelfrith. The latter was killed by the East Angles in 616 or 617, which should allow us to place the birth of their mother, and hence the reign of Cearl, sometime towards the end of the previous century. Before that we have no near-contemporary written sources for the history of the region which was to become the kingdom of Mercia, and it is not until the career of Penda, first mentioned by the Anglo-Saxon Chronicle in 626, that either the Chronicle or Bede's *History* give us anything like a continuous narrative of events there.

Nevertheless, some writers have attempted to use these few hints to construct a picture of Mercia as far back as the late sixth century. The Anglo-Saxon Chronicle identifies Penda's father as Pybba, son of Cryda, son of Cynewald. It goes on to provide Cynewald with a genealogy going back another eight generations to Woden, but we have no firm information on who most of these ancestors were, whether they were the rulers of kingdoms, or where they were located. Perhaps significantly, Cearl is not among them. Substantial portions of this family tree may of course have been concocted with the deliberate aim of conferring legitimacy, and Penda could have been eligible as a member of the royal family even if he was not directly descended from previous kings. Bede calls him 'a warrior of the Mercian royal house', but this vague description does admit the possibility that he was not a legitimate heir, and had seized the throne by force.

Henry of Huntingdon may have had an independent source, now lost, for his assertion that the Mercian kingdom was founded by Cryda about 585, and that Pybba reigned after him, followed by Cearl. If that is correct, perhaps it was Cearl who was the usurper, and Penda was merely reclaiming a throne that was his by right. In fact the word 'Cearl' may be an insult rather than a name: it seems clearly linked to the term 'ceorl' or 'churl', which in Anglo-Saxon law codes had come to denote a man of low birth. One other member of Penda's family tree, Cynewald's grandfather Icel, seems to have been a historical figure. In Felix's *Life of Saint Guthlac* we are told that the saint, who died in 714, was descended from a line of Mercian kings, 'back to Icel in whom it began in days of old', and around the time of Guthlac's death the royal dynasty began to refer to itself as the Iclingas, or people of Icel. Calculating five generations back from Penda might place Icel around the beginning of the sixth century, but although he may have been the leader of the people who later founded the kingdom, he was not a king of Mercia itself. His name is an unusual one, and it has been plausibly suggested that several surviving place names incorporating the element 'Icel' – including Ickelford in Hertfordshire and Ickleton in Cambridgeshire – were associated with him or his family (Myres). These are mostly located in Middle and East Anglia, which implies that even if the Mercians themselves were mainly indigenous, their ruling clan had originally come from the south-east. However, other place name evidence hints at a connection with what is now Worcestershire, where places such as Pedmore ('Pybba's Moor') near Stourbridge, and Pendiford ('Penda's Ford') in King's Norton, if they do not actually commemorate Penda and his forebears, at least show that their names were familiar in the region (N. Brooks, in Bassett).

Contemporary evidence suggests that even at the end of the first quarter of the seventh century, Mercia hardly existed as a recognisable entity. The Northumbrians and East Anglians seem to have been able to campaign over its territory without any interference from local forces. The first mention of Penda in the Winchester manuscript of the Chronicle, under the year 626, states that he 'had the kingdom for thirty years', but does not name the kingdom or the people over whom he ruled. The Peterborough version refers to Penda several times, but the first mention of a title appears in 645, with a reference to 'King Penda', again of an unspecified kingdom (though Bede, describing the same events with hindsight some seventy years later, does call him 'king of the Mercians'). In the Peterborough Chronicle under the year 641 he is 'Penda the Southumbrian', obviously so named in opposition to his enemy Oswald of Northumbria. The first clear statement pointing to the identity of Penda's realm comes after his death in 654, when his son Peada 'succeeded to the kingdom of the Mercians.'

The Northumbrian Menace

Whatever his formal title, for nearly thirty years after 626 Penda was the dominant figure in British affairs. The Anglo-Saxon Chronicle states under this year that he was 50 years old when he came to power, but this must be an error as his sister, who was presumably roughly his contemporary, was not married until the 640s, and Penda's own sons Peada and Wulfhere are described as young men in the following decade. More likely he was in his twenties in 626, and hence around 50, rather than 80, when he died in battle in 654.

Penda's career of conquest had its roots in a dispute between two of Mercia's more powerful neighbours, Northumbria and East Anglia. At the beginning of the seventh century the Angles north of the Humber were still divided between their two original kingdoms – Deira in the south, with its heartland in what are now the Yorkshire Wolds, and Bernicia further north. Aethelfrith, the king of Bernicia from 593 to 616, was an aggressive warlord who, according to Bede, 'ravaged the Britons more cruelly than all other English leaders.' In 603 he defeated the Scottish king Aedan in a famous battle at Degsastan, and two years later was responsible for the deaths of the 'countless number of Welsh' which the Anglo-Saxon Chronicle says were killed at Chester. His expansionist aims, however, were not directed exclusively against the British. At some point early in his reign he married the daughter of the recently deceased Aelle, king of Deira, and incorporated his southern neighbour into a united kingdom, soon to become known as Northumbria.

Aelle, however, had also left a son, Edwin, who had escaped into exile for fear that Aethelfrith would have him murdered as a potential rival. Edwin features prominently in Bede's history because of his later role in spreading Christianity in Northumbria, and the chronicler relates how he wandered incognito through 'many lands and kingdoms', always just one step ahead of Aethelfrith's assassins. As discussed above, there is evidence that he spent part of his exile in Mercia, but Cearl was probably not strong enough to resist pressure from Aethelfrith. It has even been suggested that Cearl fought against the Northumbrians at Chester in 605 and was killed there, but this is guesswork. Eventually Edwin was either forced to leave Mercia or decided to do so for his own safety, moving on to East Anglia where King Raedwald made him welcome at his court.

When news of Edwin's whereabouts reached Northumbria, Aethelfrith sent messengers to Raedwald with a bribe to induce him to kill his guest. The king at first refused, but the Northumbrians persisted, offering greater rewards, and at the same time threatening war if the fugitive was not disposed of or handed over. From subsequent events it seems that Aethelfrith backed up his threats by advancing southwards with an army, deep into what was to become Mercian territory. Eventually Raedwald, perhaps intimidated by Aethelfrith's warlike reputation, agreed to comply, but one of Edwin's friends at court informed him of the plan. Bede tells how the young prince refused to flee – believing that there was nowhere left where he would be safe, he prepared to meet his fate. In his misery he was visited by a spirit who promised that he would not only escape with his life, but would go on to become the greatest king there had ever been among the English people. In return Edwin agreed to follow the advice of whoever would help him to victory. He soon discovered that he had been saved by the intervention of Raedwald's queen, who argued that for a king to betray a guest, especially for material reward, would be to sacrifice 'the most valuable of all possessions', his royal honour.

Raedwald therefore decided on an aggressive policy, mustered his forces and struck at the Northumbrians without warning. The two armies met on the east bank of the River Idle, a tributary of the Trent, diverted in the seventeenth century, which once flowed as far north as Hatfield Chase near Doncaster. Bede describes the site as in Mercian territory, but there is no indication that the Mercians took any part in the battle. It is not unlikely that Aethelfrith had been expecting local reinforcements, but the speed of the East Anglian onslaught gave him no time to concentrate his forces. According to Bede he was greatly outnumbered by Raedwald's men, but the battle must nevertheless have been hard fought. Henry of Huntingdon's account has the East Angles advancing 'in three bodies, with fluttering standards'. The ferocious Aethelfrith allegedly launched a desperate charge against the division led by Raedwald's son Raegenhere, routing it and killing its commander. However, Raedwald stood firm in the face of this disaster, and the Northumbrian king became separated from his main body while pressing home the attack on the remaining two columns. He was surrounded and fought to the death, finally falling on top of a heap of East Anglian corpses slain by his own hand. The Northumbrians were decisively defeated and, as is customary in medieval battle narratives, the river 'was stained with English blood' (Henry of Huntingdon).

Nevertheless some sort of negotiated peace must have followed, because the former refugee Edwin suddenly found himself returning home at the head of the survivors of the army which had been sent to kill him. Aethelfrith's seven sons were in turn forced into exile among the Picts and Scots, and Edwin succeeded to the throne. The Anglo-Saxon Chronicle dates these events to the year 617, and goes on to say that the new king, apparently uninhibited by any sense of gratitude towards his East Anglian hosts, 'conquered all Britain except for the inhabitants of Kent.'

This last statement is obviously an exaggeration, but Edwin did enthusiastically continue his predecessor's expansionist foreign policy, and, according to Bede, he achieved a pre-eminence 'unmatched by any previous English king'. He annexed the little kingdom of Elmet south of the Humber, occupied the Isle of Man and launched a damaging invasion of the North Welsh kingdom of Gwynedd, during which he overran Anglesey and unsuccessfully besieged the king of Gwynedd, Cadwallon, at Priestholm.

Edwin also intervened in Wessex heavy-handedly enough to make himself unpopular, as Bede tells the story of how Cwichelm, one of several contemporary 'kings' of the West Saxons, sent an assassin named Eumer to kill him. In Bede's account this act set off a train of events which had enormous unforeseen consequences. Eumer arrived at the Northumbrian court beside the River Derwent on Easter Day 626, claiming to have an important message from Cwichelm. Edwin granted him an audience, whereupon Eumer produced a hidden dagger and attempted to stab him. One of the king's thegns, Lilla, threw himself in front of his master, but the blow was so powerful that the dagger went right through him and wounded Edwin. The king's guards quickly closed in on Eumer, but he fought so desperately that he killed another thegn named Forthhere before he was finally cut down. Bede says that the assassin's dagger was poisoned, but if so it was not very effective, as Edwin made a swift recovery from his wound.

This was an eventful day for the Northumbrian ruler, for at the same time his wife Ethelberga was giving birth to a daughter. Ethelberga was the sister of King Eadbald of Kent, and a Christian. At her brother's insistence she had been accompanied to the still-pagan Northumbrian court by an Italian bishop named Paulinus, who now lost no time in persuading Edwin that his survival and Ethelberga's painless childbirth had been due to the prayers of the queen and her Christian followers. According to Bede the king recalled his other miraculous escape at the East Anglian court, and told the bishop that if God would grant him victory over those who had tried to murder him he would in return abandon his pagan deities. He then invaded Wessex and was victorious, killing five 'kings' and countless other people. Bede says that he killed or captured all those who had been involved in the assassination plot, although this cannot have included Cwichelm himself, who was still in power two years later.

'Not Angles but Angels'
Despite this apparent sign from heaven Edwin remained reluctant to commit himself to Christianity, and Bede quotes letters sent to

him and Ethelberga by Pope Boniface V, at Paulinus' instigation, encouraging him to take the final step. It was during this period that one of his councillors made perhaps the most famous speech of the age, likening the life of a man to the flight of a sparrow through a firelit hall on a winter's night, from the darkness, briefly into the light, then back into darkness. Any teaching that could shed light on what happened before or after our short span on earth, he argued, was worth following. Edwin may of course have been genuinely interested in religious matters, and Bede, anxious to establish him as one of the first and greatest of English saints, would have us believe so. But Christianity also had practical advantages, not least in promising diplomatic and trade contacts with the already converted peoples of south-eastern England and the Continent, and in providing access to the services of literate churchmen such as Paulinus with experience of Roman legal and administrative practices.

We know very little about post-Roman English paganism, but we can be sure that by the 620s it was increasingly beleaguered. Much of the west of Britain had retained an unbroken tradition of Christianity since Roman times, and during the fifth and sixth centuries, when the faith had been giving ground in England, it continued to spread westwards. Receiving their Christianity from Palladius and Patrick in the late fifth century, the Irish had re-exported it to the Picts and Scots of Scotland in the sixth. Meanwhile, across the English Channel the Franks, a warlike German people who had overrun much of Roman Gaul, had been converted under their king Clovis in 496. How much of the religion persisted in England is unclear, but Bede admits that the Hwicce were already converted by the time missionaries from Rome reached the area, and records that the first of these missionaries, Augustine, found a church already available for use when he arrived in Kent in 597. This mission was sent by Pope Gregory, whose interest in the plight of the heathen English was said to have been inspired by the sight of Anglian slave boys in the market at Rome, the subjects of his famous pun, 'non Anglii sed Angeli'.

At first Augustine and his companions were reluctant to venture among what Bede calls 'a barbarous, fierce and pagan nation', but they need not have worried. King Aethelberht of Kent was already disposed towards toleration because his wife Bertha, a Frankish princess, was a Christian. By the time of his death in 616 Aethelberht himself had accepted baptism. The teachings of Augustine and his followers were soon gaining, or regaining, ground across most of England, thanks to the Roman missionaries' tactic of converting the rulers first and encouraging them to set an example to their people.

Bede ascribes the conversion of the West Saxons to the year 635, and adds that at about the same time the throne of the East Angles, whose ruling family had fluctuated in their allegiance to the new faith during the reign of King Raedwald, was occupied by Sigeberht, 'a good and religious man' who had been baptised while living in exile in France during Raedwald's reign, and who now requested a bishop to be sent from Canterbury to consolidate the East Anglian church. Five years later the newly crowned King Eorconberht of Kent was the first English ruler to prohibit paganism, order the destruction of idols, and introduce compulsory fasting during Lent. Christianity was no longer a matter purely of personal conviction but was becoming a state ideology, in aggressive opposition to the remnants of the ancient religion of the Angles and Saxons.

Only Mercia continued to resist the wave of conversion. Even Bede admits, however, that Penda was no diehard pagan fanatic. He refused to accept baptism himself, but he tolerated those who preached Christianity to his subjects and allowed his own sons to convert. In fact he reserved his scorn for those who professed to follow the new faith but failed to live up to its ideals. For this reason it is unlikely that religion was an important motive behind his wars, at least on the Mercian side. This, however, did not prevent the chronicler and many of those who followed him from stigmatising the Mercians as irreconcilable pagans, often referring to them as 'the heathen', in contrast to the nominally Christian armies of their rivals. Unfortunately our sources for the pre-Christian beliefs of the English are too poor to enable us to reconstruct the role of religion in motivating their armies, and it is likely that there never was a coherent 'pagan' theology, but rather a loosely organised collection of gods and beliefs varying from place to place. Bede's account of the conversion of Edwin's Northumbria suggests that by the seventh century even its own priests were losing faith in the ability of the old gods to deliver victory, but Bede is hardly an unbiased source.

Bede also tells us that pagan priests were not allowed to bear arms or to ride stallions, but this need not preclude a ceremonial or morale-boosting role on the battlefield. There is plenty of evidence that Christian commanders made use of crosses, prayer and similar devices to encourage their troops, and Bede's description of the Battle of Chester in 605 suggests that non-Christians may also have believed in the efficacy of such tactics. Faced with an invasion by Aethelfrith's Northumbrians, the Britons of North Wales recruited a contingent of over 1,200 priests, mostly brought from the great monastery at Bangor, to pray for victory. These were drawn up separately from the British army in what was supposed to be a safe location, and were provided with a bodyguard led by a man named Brocmail or Scrocmail. But before the battle began they were spotted by Aethelfrith, who asked his advisers who they were. On being informed of their identity he declared that 'if they are crying to their God against us, they are fighting against us even if they do not bear arms.' He therefore ordered the first attack to be made not against the enemy army, but against the Christian holy men. Brocmail and his warriors, who had no doubt thought that their duties would keep them safely out of danger, ran away and left their charges to be massacred. The Northumbrians then wheeled against the British main body and destroyed it after a hard fight.

It is tempting to play down the Christian/heathen dichotomy which runs through Bede's writings as a product of his own religious background, and to question whether it was as important to the people of early seventh-century England as it seemed with hindsight. But this was not just a matter of doctrine and personal conviction: the visible manifestations of the two religious traditions could be very different indeed. There were pagan practices in Britain – whether ancient survivals or new introductions – which would have struck a contemporary Christian as barbarous in the extreme. The excavations at Sutton Hoo in the 1980s revealed that the mounds where the East Anglian kings were presumably buried were accompanied by two groups of burials consisting of bodies which had been dismembered in various ways before being placed in the ground. Many of these 'execution burials' clearly dated from the Christian era and so are likely to represent victims of judicial punishment, but at least some of the earlier ones can be interpreted as human sacrifices. Perhaps the sinister associations of the site persisted for several centuries, making it seem a suitable spot for the execution and burial of criminals.

The obvious parallel, drawn by the excavators of Sutton Hoo themselves, was with Sweden, where the East Anglian royal dynasty, the Wuffingas, believed itself to have originated (Carver). The missionary Adam of Bremen visited Uppsala in the ninth century, and has left a gruesome account of the pagan rituals performed there. The central feature was a temple, decorated in gold, where statues representing the gods Thor, Woden and Frey were worshipped, along with lesser 'heroes made gods', whose exploits on earth were thought to have earned them immortality. Apart from routine sacrifices offered by the priests to celebrate marriages, for relief from disease or hunger or for success in war, a great ceremony was held at Uppsala every nine years. Each day for nine days a man was executed, apparently by decapitation, his blood offered to the gods, and his body hung on a tree until it rotted. Male animals, including dogs and horses, were killed to accompany each human sacrifice. Adam reports with horror that attendance at this ceremony was compulsory, even for Christian converts, and says that one Christian told him that he had seen seventy-two bodies in various stages of putrefaction hanging from the trees of the sacred grove.

If the early kings of Mercia ever had a burial complex like Sutton Hoo no trace of it has been found, but it is not impossible that such a ritual centre lay at the heart of Cearl's or Penda's realm. No pagan temple has been definitely identified from the Anglo-Saxon period in England, but from Bede's account of the Northumbrians burning theirs it seems that they were often built of wood, and so would not have survived even if they were not deliberately demolished. Pope Gregory, writing to Abbot Mellitus in 601, directed that if temples

63

were 'well built' they should not be destroyed but purified and converted into churches; if this was common practice many pre-Christian temples must lie underneath existing churches, although there seems so far to be little, if any, archaeological proof of this.

Penda and Cadwallon

Unfortunately for Edwin his eventual conversion brought him few earthly rewards, and if the Tribal Hidage does represent his idea of the tribute owed to him it is highly unlikely that he lived to collect it. Bede describes the well-ordered and peaceful life of his kingdom during the period when he 'laboured for the kingdom of Christ,' and the concern which he showed for his subjects' well being, even providing brass bowls on posts beside the springs along the highways so that travellers could drink. Nevertheless, his career of conquest had made him many enemies, and in the vast debatable land to the south forces were beginning to stir – perhaps even brought into being by his and his predecessor's ruthless campaigning in the area – which were to destroy him.

Penda's first recorded campaign took place in 628, when he fought a battle at Cirencester against the West Saxons Cynegils and Cwichelm. Cirencester, on the northern frontier of West Saxon territory, might have seemed an easy target, for it had only been in Saxon hands for fifty years and its allegiance may still have been uncertain. If this was Penda's assessment, however, he was mistaken. The Anglo-Saxon Chronicle gives no further details of the battle, except that afterwards the combatants made an agreement, which suggests that the fighting had been inconclusive. Henry of Huntingdon says that the commanders on both sides had taken an oath not to retreat, but neither could gain the advantage and the armies broke off the fighting at sunset with a sense of relief. The next morning Penda and the West Saxons agreed to make peace in order to avoid mutual destruction. Cirencester itself, along with the rest of the country north of the Thames, passed into the possession of the Hwicce, which implies that Penda had the upper hand. He next appears in the sources in 633, by which time he had switched his attention to the Northumbrian frontier.

King Cadwallon of Gwynedd had, in Bede's words, 'rebelled' against Edwin, though the latter's overlordship of North Wales may never have been more than nominal. Certainly the previous quarter century of Northumbrian attacks on the Welsh would seem to provide plenty of justification for Cadwallon's hostility, but from Bede's Northumbrian perspective he was an unmitigated villain. 'A barbarian more savage than any pagan', says the chronicler, '... although he professed to call himself a Christian, he was utterly barbarous in temperament and behaviour.' Bede was undoubtedly prejudiced against the Britons, but we have some confirmation of his view from the Welsh themselves. The 'Marwnad Cynddylan', or 'Lament for Cynddylan', relates the exploits of Cynddylan ap Cyndrwyn, who was king of Gwynedd's southern neighbour Powys in the early seventh century and, like Cadwallon, was an ally of Penda. The poem is known only from a seventeenth-century copy, but it is believed to have been originally composed not long after its subject's death (Rowland).

Probably at some point prior to his alliance with the Mercians, Cynddylan had led a raid on a place known in Welsh as Caer Lwytgoed, which is generally identified with Lichfield, although at that time the settlement was probably still at the site of the nearby Roman ruins at Wall. As Professor Brooks has pointed out, the name 'Caer' implies a fortification or at least a defended camp, but there are no traces of such defences at Lichfield at this date, and Bede's account of Saint Chad's arrival there in the 660s implies that the site was then uninhabited.

At Wall, however, Roman walls twelve feet high were still to be seen in the eighteenth century, and 1,000 years earlier they may still have been a formidable obstacle. It seems very likely, in fact, that Wall was the site of Penda's capital in the early days of the kingdom. The Welsh hero of the attack on this place, we are told, not only carried off 'fifteen hundred cattle' and 'four twenties of stallions', but also attacked the 'wretched bishop' and the 'book-keeping monks'. Relations between the English and Welsh Churches were bitterly hostile at this time. Bede tells us that the Welsh clergy refused even to eat from a vessel that an Englishman had touched,

65

while retaliating by suggesting that the massacre of the Welsh priests at Chester in 605 was God's punishment for rejecting the authority of Augustine and his Roman mission.

The nature of Welsh armies in the early Middle Ages is difficult to reconstruct from the scanty sources, but they probably resembled their twelfth- and thirteenth-century descendants in being lightly armed, and better equipped for fighting in mountainous terrain than the English. In his discussion of the Saxon siege of the camp at Andredecester (probably Pevensey in Sussex) in 491, Henry of Huntingdon inserts a discussion of British tactics which, while reminiscent of those of his own contemporaries, is not obviously anachronistic for the fifth century. He says that the Britons outside the camp 'swarmed together like wasps,' harassing the Saxons with hit-and-run attacks, shooting from a distance with bows and slings and luring them into ambushes in the woods, where, being 'lighter of foot', they had the advantage.

Henry's description of the Battle of Beranbyrg, fought according to the Anglo-Saxon Chronicle between the Britons and the West Saxons in 556, also contrasts the British tactics with those of the Saxons. The latter attacked in a single compact body, while the Britons drew up in 'nine battalions, a convenient number for military tactics, three being posted in the van, three in the centre, and three in the rear, with chosen commanders for each, while the archers and slingers and cavalry were disposed after the Roman order'. This last comment probably means with the cavalry on the wings and the missile troops shooting overhead from a rear rank, as was the practice in the later Roman legions. It is hard to know whether this account preserves a genuine tradition or is based on the tactics of the twelfth century, when Henry was writing, but it is interesting that he attributes to the Britons a deployment which in his own day was associated with the Anglo-Norman armies rather than the Welsh. Henry's account of contemporary Welsh soldiers at the Battle of Lincoln describes them as armed only with knives, lacking order and unable to stand up to cavalry.

Gerald of Wales, who wrote around the 1180s, described his countrymen as armed with very long spears, which they threw like javelins as they attacked. Their first onslaught was delivered with reckless ferocity and appeared formidable, but if they were once thrown back they quickly fell into confusion. They never attempted to counterattack after a repulse, but instead fled without attempting to rally. Therefore their battles were nearly always won or lost as a result of a single charge. The Welsh preferred rough or marshy ground, no doubt because it hampered them less in their manoeuvres than it did more heavily armed opponents. In fact their main aim in warfare was not to kill their enemies, but to acquire booty. The famous Welsh archers existed in Gerald's day, but – leaving Henry of Huntingdon's story aside – do not seem to be mentioned before the early twelfth century. It has been pointed out that the Welsh word for 'bow' is derived from English, which suggests that it was not a traditional weapon.

The warriors of Gwynedd in the eleventh century are described as relying on swords and shields, which would obviously be the most appropriate weapons for a headlong charge to close quarters. The heroes of the epic Welsh saga 'Mabinogion' fight on horseback, as do those of the poem 'Y Gododdin', which is believed to describe a mounted attack on Northumbria in the late sixth century. It is often suggested that British cavalry tactics reflect the surviving influence of the late Roman army, and it is true that Gildas states that the departing Romans left their former subjects patterns for manufacturing weapons (Heath). However, the Picts, who had never been conquered by the Romans, also made extensive use of cavalry, which suggests that it was an indigenous development.

Under Cadwallon the Welsh did not confine themselves to defending what was now regarded as British territory, but carried the fight deep into England in alliance with their Mercian neighbours. At this point the Mercian leader seems to have been the junior partner in this alliance; Matthew of Westminster has an unlikely story that Cadwallon had captured Penda when the latter was besieging Exeter, and forced him to swear allegiance, though how or why a Mercian king would have been campaigning in the far south-west of England is not explained. At any rate their combined forces brought Edwin to battle on 12 October 633 at a place which

Bede calls Haethfelth. The site is usually identified with Hatfield Chase near Doncaster, but this seems to derive from no earlier authority than William Camden, who in his *Britannia* of 1586 based his argument on the similarity of the place names and a tradition that there had once been an Anglo-Saxon hall there. It has been suggested that this would have been a good place for an ambush, as the road from Lindsey to York was forced by surrounding marshes to pass through a narrow gap where an army could be trapped against the River Don, and that the allies might have been lying in wait for Edwin there (Higham, 1995). It may also have been close to the site of the River Idle battle between Raedwald and Aethelfrith. However, there is an alternative site thirty miles further south, near Edwinstowe in Sherwood Forest, where there are traces of a cult of Edwin in the later Middle Ages. An undated mass grave was found near St Mary's Church at Cuckney, five miles to the north-west of Edwinstowe, in 1951. It was unearthed when the National Coal Board was carrying out work to reinforce the foundations of the church and was not investigated by professional archaeologists, but it was said to contain the skeletons of more than 200 young men (Barley). A Norman castle once existed on the site of the present cemetery at Cuckney, but as bodies would hardly be buried inside an inhabited castle it is probable that the remains are earlier. It may also be significant that an area known locally as Hatfield Chase still exists in the vicinity.

The Edwinstowe district is situated in what later became known as Sherwood Forest, and the name 'Haethfelth' or 'Heath Field' may denote a relatively open area in the middle of the forest in which the Mercian army might have deployed to await the Northumbrians. We know nothing of the course of the fighting, except that the 48-year-old Edwin was killed, together with his son Osfrith, a 'gallant young warrior' who fell before his father, perhaps leading the Northumbrian vanguard. Edwin's army was routed, and another royal prince, Eadfrith, was captured by Penda, who promised to spare his life in return for his submission but later broke his word and executed him. The allies then marched north through Northumbria with fire and sword, a rampage which Bede's informants clearly remembered with horror a century later. Cadwallon, he says, planned to exterminate the entire English race, showing no respect for churches, and putting even women and children to 'horrible deaths'. The fact that Cadwallon's closest ally was an Angle suggests that this genocidal policy was an exaggeration, but this does seem to have been more than the customary pillaging raid.

Edwin's chaplain Bishop Paulinus declined the chance of martyrdom at the hands of either Mercian pagans or Welsh heretics, but instead smuggled Queen Ethelberga and her children onto a ship and fled with them to Kent, where her father gave them shelter and Paulinus took over the safe bishopric of Rochester. Also rescued were some of the kingdom's famous treasures, including a great golden cross and chalice which were still in Canterbury in Bede's day. The Northumbrian kingdom was temporarily overrun. Deira seceded under a cousin of Edwin named Osric, while Eanfrith, one of Aethelfrith's sons, returned to take over in Bernicia. But Cadwallon and Penda continued their attacks. In the summer of 634 Osric besieged Cadwallon in a stronghold which Bede does not name, but the Welsh king brought out his entire force and took him by surprise. Osric was killed and his army annihilated. Soon afterwards Eanfrith arrived in the Welsh camp, accompanied by only twelve companions, to discuss peace terms. His motive for this rash act is not explained, but Cadwallon was in no mood to negotiate and had him killed. Bede, ignoring the equally tragic fate of his hero Edwin, attributes the downfall of Osric and Eanfrith to the fact that they had both abandoned Christianity, and says that later historical tradition disregarded their brief reigns on this account, and ascribed the year 634 to that of their successor, Eanfrith's brother Oswald.

Oswald was a Christian, and astutely capitalised on this to motivate his warriors, no doubt demoralised by the disastrous failure of their most recent leaders. At some point Cadwallon appears to have become separated from Penda's Mercians and was campaigning on the northern side of Hadrian's Wall, not far from Hexham. At the time the frontier with the Picts and Scots had been pushed far to the north, thanks to the campaigns of Aethelfrith and Edwin, and the country along the wall seems to have been more intensively farmed than it is now, perhaps a legacy from the Roman military occupation. The Welsh king was therefore operating in a productive and so far unravaged landscape which may have been well worth plundering, but this move put him a long way from the support of his ally. Oswald caught him at a place called Denisesburn, a site still well known in Bede's day as a place of pilgrimage. Even though their enemies had split their forces the Northumbrians were badly outnumbered: 'small in numbers', says Bede, 'but strong in the faith of Christ'. Oswald had a large cross made and planted in a hole in the ground, then gathered the whole army around it to kneel in prayer. After this they drew up in battle order and advanced on the enemy 'at the first light of dawn'. This implies that they may have had the advantage of surprise against a still-sleeping opponent, but Bede gives no more details except that Cadwallon was killed in what was clearly a serious defeat for the Welsh. The exact site of the encounter is difficult to determine because places traditionally associated with it lie both north and south of Hadrian's Wall, but this might be explained if the Welsh had suffered most of their casualties in a running fight as they attempted to retreat southwards.

'The Heathen'

Penda's army was not involved in this disaster, but the Mercians may not yet have felt strong enough to fight on alone. We hear no more of the struggle on their northern frontier for eight years, during which Oswald seems to have devoted himself to consolidation at home, and to the importation of missionaries from Scotland to complete the conversion of his people and re-establish the organisation of his shattered church.

Penda's next victim was Raedwald's son Sigeberht, the pious young man whom Bede praised for his role in the establishment of Christianity in East Anglia. After ruling his kingdom for a while he decided to abdicate and enter a monastery, handing over power to a relative named Egric. When faced with a Mercian invasion sometime in the late 630s the East Angles soon realised that they were outclassed, and called on Sigeberht, who had been a famous warrior in his youth, to come back and lead them. He at first refused, but was forcibly dragged from his monastery and obliged to accompany Egric's army when it marched out to meet Penda. Sigeberht would not abandon his monastic vows and refused to carry any weapons except for a stick, but his people apparently hoped that his mere presence would steady the morale of the army. In the event it was not enough. 'When the heathen charged', says Bede, both Sigeberht and Egric were killed in the inevitable rout. They were succeeded by a nobleman called Anna, who held onto power intermittently for almost another two decades before he too faced Penda in battle.

In the summer of 642 the Mercian–Northumbrian war resumed. There may of course have been small-scale campaigns and border skirmishes during the years since Cadwallon's death, but the chroniclers do not mention them. Nor do they discuss any possible motive for a new outbreak of hostilities. There is a strong sense behind the laconic notices in Bede and the Anglo-Saxon Chronicle that under Penda Mercia was responsible for a reign of terror throughout the country. All of the older, more settled and increasingly Christianised kingdoms of the south, east and north-east were looking uneasily towards the turbulent interior of the island, where no bishop had yet ventured and pagan barbarism still seemed to reign. To be killed or driven out by Penda was almost the expected fate for their kings. Oswald met his doom at the age of 38, on 5 August 642, when he encountered the 'heathen' at a place known to Bede as Maserfelth or Maserfeld. Bede refers to a 'fierce battle', but no details of the fighting survive. Penda's brother Eowa was killed there, which has led to speculation that he was fighting against Penda in the Northumbrian army, but his death does not necessarily imply that he was on the losing side (Brooks). Henry of Huntingdon quotes an anonymous source as describing how after the battle 'the plain at Mesafeld [sic] was whitened with the bones of saints' – in other words the Christian Northumbrians, elevated to the status of martyrs by their deaths at heathen hands.

The site of this encounter is usually supposed to be near Oswestry in Shropshire, which would imply a Northumbrian invasion of

Mercian territory, but this identification is controversial. It seems to have been first suggested by Reginald of Durham in his *Life of Saint Oswald*, written in the late twelfth century. Reginald says that the site of the king's death was marked by an ash tree at a place still known then as Maserfeld, a location that pilgrims continued to visit in his day. This seems inherently plausible, even though the name Maserfeld has now disappeared, because it is generally agreed that Oswestry derives from the Old English Oswaldstreow or 'Oswald's Tree', the Welsh version being Croesoswald, or 'Oswald's Cross'. The battle itself was known in Welsh poetry as Maes Cogwy, and to Nennius, writing in Latin, as Bellum Cocboy, but no modern equivalent has been located. Other suggestions place the battle further north, in or near to Northumbrian territory, which would mean that rather than taking the fight to the enemy, Oswald was conducting a defensive campaign against yet another Mercian invasion. Bede refers to him as being killed 'fighting for his country against the heathen', though he would be expected to portray his hero's death in the best possible light, and in any case an invasion of Mercia could have had a defensive purpose, perhaps to pre-empt an expected attack and ensure that this time it was Penda's lands rather than Oswald's that were ravaged by the campaigning armies. Another candidate for the battle site is in Lancashire, where the church at Winwick is traditionally associated with Saint Oswald, and still has a 'Saint Oswald's well' in the vicinity. The surrounding district was once known as Makerfield, and the place names Ashton- and Ince-in-Makerfield survive today south of Wigan. Unfortunately, however, there seems to be no etymological link between the names Makerfield and Maserfelth (Kenyon).

A site on the other side of the Pennines, near Bardney in Lindsey, has also recently been put forward (Clarkson). The evidence for this rests not on an account of the campaign itself, but on the subsequent fate of Oswald's remains. Bede says that after the king's death Penda had Oswald's head and forearms cut off and displayed on stakes in a gruesome pagan ritual, presumably on the battlefield itself. The next year Oswald's successor, his brother Oswy, led an army to the spot and retrieved the relics, taking the head to the monastery at Lindisfarne and the arms to Bamburgh, where the Anglo-Saxon Chronicle says that they remained uncorrupted as a sign of their former owner's sanctity. Clarkson argues that Oswy would not have been in a position to launch another major invasion of the Mercian heartland so soon after the crushing defeat of the previous year, and hence that the field must have been located within easy reach of a raiding party coming from north of the River Humber. Furthermore, at a later date Oswy's daughter Osthryth, who was then married to the Mercian king Aethelred (reigned 675– 704), located the rest of her uncle's bones and donated them to the monastery at Bardney, in modern Lincolnshire. This would have involved a gruelling and apparently unnecessary journey across England from Oswestry, but might seem more logical if Bardney had in fact been the nearest suitable location to the spot where Oswald died.

This argument, however, relies heavily on the supposed diffi- culties of overland travel in the early Middle Ages, which have often been exaggerated. Oswald's remains could have been trans- ported from Shropshire to Lindsey in, at most, a few weeks, by known highways running through territory controlled by Osthryth's husband. Bardney, far from being an illogical choice, was being promoted by Aethelred and his queen as a major religious centre. The bones of a saint would have been a valuable asset for such an establishment, conveniently tying in with Osthryth's natural desire to find a safe resting place for her famous uncle. It is interesting to note that Oswald was far from being a local hero in Lindsey. According to Bede, the monks at Bardney at first refused to accept the bones as they remembered the Northumbrian king as a foreign oppressor, and they were only persuaded of his sanctity by a convenient miracle. As far as Oswy's mission to the battlefield is concerned, it could easily have been achieved by a mounted raiding party small and mobile enough to evade any Mercian patrols and penetrate deep into the enemy's country. That the grisly relics were guarded seems unlikely: old battlefields were unpleasant places, which we know from other sources would soon have been abandoned to wolves and other scavengers, and would also probably have been avoided for health or superstitious reasons.

If Maserfelth was indeed near Oswestry – as seems most probable – its exact site has been lost, but the general location suggests a possible strategic context for the battle. The previous devastating invasion of Northumbria had been undertaken by a combined army of Mercians and Welsh, and it is possible that Oswald knew, or feared, that a similar alliance was being put together in preparation for another invasion after the harvest of 642. A logical response to such a threat would have been to advance via Chester, which may still have been in Northumbrian hands after Aethelfrith's victory in 605, and then south along the Welsh Marches with the aim of preventing the Welsh and Mercian armies linking up, ravaging the countryside from which they obtained their supplies, and perhaps catching and defeating them separately. Bede might then still have been justified in regarding this as a defensive war. Whether Oswald miscalculated and was caught between the two forces, or whether the Mercians alone proved too strong for him, we do not know, but both Bede and the Anglo-Saxon Chronicle attribute the victory solely to Penda.

In 645 it was the turn of Cenwalh of Wessex. Cenwalh was the son and successor of Penda's former enemy Cynegils, and, perhaps as part of a peace settlement, he had recently married one of Penda's sisters. Foolishly he abandoned his wife in favour of another woman, and an infuriated Penda marched south to restore the family honour. Cenwalh was obviously unable to muster an army to resist the invasion, because he was forced to flee the country and take refuge with King Anna of East Anglia. Then under the year 654 the Anglo-Saxon Chronicle records laconically that 'here King Anna was killed', almost as if there was no need to elaborate on the cause of yet another royal death in those violent years. But Bede places the blame on Penda, and Henry of Huntingdon adds that Anna and his army were slaughtered in a battle from which few survivors escaped. A possible location for this fight is at Blytheburgh, near Southwold on the coast of Suffolk, where there was a shrine in Anna's memory in the twelfth century. He was the third East Anglian king in succession to fall victim to the pagan Mercians.

The Battle of the Winwaed

Soon afterwards Penda embarked on his last campaign. He must now have been at least 50 years old, but Bede portrays him as just as bloodthirsty and eager for battle as he had ever been. He had recently led several more damaging raids into Northumbria, prompting King Oswy, Oswald's brother and successor, to offer him 'an incalculable quantity' of treasure in return for peace. But the 'treacherous' Mercian king refused to negotiate and instead announced his intention of destroying the whole Northumbrian nation, 'from the highest to the humblest in the land'. However, Bede, as always, tells only one side of the story, and it is not clear what Penda's motive could have been for such a drastic policy. More likely his grievance against Oswy stemmed from the latter's attempts to reunite the kingdoms of Bernicia and Deira, which had regained their independence after the death of Oswald. In 651 Oswy had killed Oswine, the king of Deira, but succeeded only in driving his people into the hands of the Mercians when their new ruler, Aethelwald, sought Penda's protection.

The army which Penda led northwards to put an end to Oswy's intrigues included troops from most of southern Britain. Aethelhere, who had succeeded his brother Anna as king of East Anglia only a year previously, led his own contingent, as did Cadafael ap Cynfeddw of Gwynedd and several other Welsh princes. Altogether, according to Bede, there were thirty 'battle hardened legions under famous commanders'. The Anglo-Saxon Chronicle calls these commanders 'royal children' – not necessarily all Penda's children, of course – and adds that some of them were kings in their own right. They may represent the last appearance in history of the rulers of the Noxgaga, Ciltern Saetna and other obscure 'tribes' of the Tribal Hidage, soon to lose their identity in the consolidating kingdom of Mercia. Aethelwald's Deirans provided guides for the expedition, although Bede says that they refused to take part in actual combat against their fellow Northumbrians and retired before battle was joined.

Nennius, in his *Historia Brittonum*, states that Oswy took refuge in a fortified place called Iudeu, from where he delivered all the valuables he could collect as tribute to Penda, who gave them to his Welsh allies. Iudeu has been placed as far north as Stirling in central Scotland, but this is uncertain. Nennius' version is obviously inconsistent with Bede's statement that Penda had rejected the proffered treasure, but if the Mercian leader first accepted payment and then later broke a promise to withdraw, it would account for the chronicler's description of him as 'treacherous'. Eventually Oswy realised that he had no choice but to risk a battle, even though he was heavily outnumbered – by thirty to one according to Bede. He made his stand on 15 November 654 (or possibly 655) by the River Winwaed, which cannot be precisely identified but is generally assumed to have been somewhere in what is now Yorkshire. Stenton and others place it east of Leeds, where a location near Barwick-in-Elmet, in the valley of the River Cock, is still known as Penda's Fields. Bede's narrative suggests that the Winwaed was a much more substantial river than the Cock is today, but much of the area overlies impermeable boulder clay, and it would have flooded more easily before the era of modern drainage. If this is the right location, it is near to the sites of two of the other great battlefields of English history. A few miles downstream is the field of Towton, the bloodiest encounter of the Wars of the Roses, where in 1461 the defeated Lancastrians drowned in the waters of the River Cock as the Mercians may have done eight centuries before. Ten miles further north is Marston Moor, the scene of Cromwell's triumph over Charles I in 1644. That three such decisive battles should have been fought in such a small area is more than coincidence, for this has always been the main route between the Midlands and the north. In fact the strip of territory between Mansfield and Doncaster has been aptly described as the 'cockpit' of Anglo-Saxon England, constantly fought over by Mercian armies aiming for York and Northumbrians striking southwards towards the valley of the Trent.

Unfortunately the manoeuvres which led up to the Battle of the Winwaed cannot now be reconstructed. If Penda had really marched as far as Scotland the location of the site would imply that he was on his way home, but if this was the case it is hard to see what Oswy stood to gain from obstructing him. Probably the initial contact had taken place further south, and the crossing of the Winwaed marked an attempt by the Mercians to invade the rich farming country around York at a time when the harvest would have been gathered and ready for the taking. Heavy rain had caused the river to overflow its banks and flood the surrounding area, but it appears from Bede's account that Penda must somehow have forded it and fought with his back to the water. Geoffrey of Monmouth, whose brief narrative otherwise seems to derive entirely from Bede, suggests that the Northumbrians were drawn up along the bank to contest the crossing, but Geoffrey is a late and not very reliable source, and such a deployment would have been extremely risky. More likely, perhaps, is that Oswy was planning to attack the Mercians as they tried to reform after the crossing and drive them back into the river.

Despite his strategic advantage, the Northumbrian king was understandably pessimistic: not only was Penda much stronger in numbers, but he had a formidable record of success. During the past thirty years he had never lost a major battle, and at least five kings had already met their deaths at his hands. To dare to take the field against him must have seemed literally suicide. The Northumbrian therefore decided to play the only card he had: his people's Christian religion. He made a vow that if he was victorious he would donate twelve royal estates to build monasteries, and give his infant daughter to God 'as a consecrated virgin'. He and his son Alchfrid then led their troops into battle.

Unfortunately we have no details of the fighting, but the result was an unprecedented disaster for the Mercians. To Bede the Northumbrian victory required no further explanation than 'the mercy of God', and this may not have been far from the truth. History provides other examples of a tiny outnumbered force, reduced to the courage of despair and inspired by its faith, sweeping all before it: the Crusaders at Antioch, for example, or the Northumbrians themselves at Denisesburn. By contrast, Penda's army was linguistically and religiously diverse, and we do not know what tensions might have arisen among the various contingents. The presence of thirty leaders, some of whom were kings in their own right, must have greatly complicated the business of command. Some of them deserted at the last moment, including Cadafael, who according to Nennius earned the nickname of 'battle-shirker' for his behaviour on that day.

The differing versions of the fate of Oswy's treasure might possibly stem from a secret deal struck with the Welsh princes, or perhaps they were becoming reluctant to fight for a pagan ally against their fellow Christians. Others in Penda's army, even though they had no obvious reason for loyalty, stood and fought to the end. Bede records that the East Angles and their king, Anna's brother Aethelhere, were killed to a man. Penda himself, the grizzled veteran of thirty years of victorious warfare, is unlikely to have thought of retreat, or to have expected mercy. We can imagine him fighting on grimly in the front rank, trying again and again to rally the waverers by the force of his personality, calling on Woden and the other pagan gods – if he still believed in them – to curse his enemies as the Christian banners closed in around him. Henry of Huntingdon imaginatively claims that Penda's nerve failed him at the end, when he discovered that his enemies had at last learned to stand up to him, and 'he who had shed the blood of others now suffered what he had inflicted on them.' Eventually he fell, and his army broke in rout. However, the flooded river lay between the Mercians and safety, and Bede says that, as often happened in medieval warfare, more men died by drowning while attempting to cross it than had been killed on the battlefield itself.

In the immediate aftermath of his victory at the Winwaed, Oswy claimed a brief overlordship over the whole of Mercia. Penda was succeeded by his son Peada, who, says the Anglo-Saxon Chronicle, 'ruled no length of time, because he was betrayed by his own queen at Eastertide.' Bede's account is slightly different, because he states that for three years Oswy himself replaced Penda as the direct ruler of Mercia, and that Peada ruled only the 'Kingdom of the Middle Angles' – a country of 5,000 hides which was clearly an artificial creation imposed by the victorious Northumbrians – as a vassal and son-in-law of Oswy.

Chapter 5

Two Treasures

On two different occasions during the tumultuous half century described in the previous chapter, in different parts of the country, people placed in the ground treasures which were to remain buried for more than 1,300 years. When they finally emerged, in 1939 and seventy years later, they provided the distant descendants of those anonymous Anglo-Saxons with stunning evidence of the glory of kings such as Penda, who had until then been no more than names in the chronicles.

The 'Sutton Hoo Man'

The first of these discoveries was made in the kingdom of Raedwald of the East Angles, whose victory at the River Idle had been a catalyst for the Mercian Wars. The barrows or burial mounds which stood on a windswept rise overlooking the River Deben, at Sutton Hoo on the Suffolk coast, had been recognised for what they are as long ago as the sixteenth century, and sporadic attempts had been made ever since to excavate them, or rather to dig them up in the hunt for buried treasure. However, the treasure seekers had missed the greatest prize, as became apparent in 1938–9 when the land-owner, Mrs Edith Pretty, commissioned a local archaeologist to excavate them scientifically. In May 1939 the biggest barrow, which became known as Mound One, proved to contain the remains of a wooden ship, underneath which was an intact burial chamber. The sandy soil was very acidic and little organic material had survived – at first there appeared to be no sign of a body, although traces of phosphate residues have since been found which indicate that human remains had been interred there (Carver).

The items which were found, however, were enough to revolutionise the study of the period. As Professor Martin Carver put it, 'Every Dark Age object that had been imagined, and a few that had not, seemed to be represented.' Another seventeen barrows have since been excavated, but Mound One remains the most spectacular, the site associated in the popular imagination with the words 'Sutton Hoo'. The ship survived only as rusted rivets and an impression in the sand, but it appeared to have been a fully seaworthy vessel, about ninety feet long and carrying a crew of forty oarsmen. Other finds included cauldrons, lamps, drinking horns, gold coins and jewellery, some coming from as far afield as Constantinople. The deceased had also been buried with his complete war panoply, comprising a coat of mail, a sword, shield, spears, gold- and garnet-decorated shoulder clasps and fittings for belts and scabbards, as well as, of course, the famous helmet. The latter, as restored at the British Museum with its full face mask and elaborate tinned bronze decoration, has become the best-known image of the era, instantly recognisable worldwide as a symbol of Anglo-Saxon wealth and power.

Also in the tomb were some objects whose function was far from obvious. One, a long whetstone decorated with bronze fittings, has become popularly known as the 'sceptre', and is certainly impressive enough to have been a symbol of rank. It does not appear to have actually been used for sharpening weapons, but the symbolism of a war leader having such a thing on show in his hall, ready for emergencies, seems obvious. Even more mysterious is the iron 'standard'. As restored, this is basically an iron rod just over four feet in height, with a cross-shaped piece of metal on the top and a larger grid just below it. The other end has a point with two scrolls above it, obviously designed to be placed either in the ground or in some sort of socket. The piece has been variously interpreted as a standard, a rack for holding torches, or even as a scalp-pole on which a pagan king might display the trophies of his dead enemies. More prosaically it looks rather like a hat-stand, and it is quite possible that that is what it was. The Sutton Hoo helmet, with its intimidating face mask, may well have been as iconic a symbol of its owner in his lifetime as it is today, and it is surely more likely to have been displayed on a prominent stand in his hall, out of the way of damp, vermin and accidental damage, than to have been simply hung on the wall or kept out of sight in a box.

Whatever their purpose, items such as these, and the general richness of the grave, led immediately to speculation that the deceased had been a king, possibly one eminent enough to have been recorded in historical sources. It was known from Bede that the district of Sutton Hoo had once been part of the kingdom of East Anglia, and the style of the coins and other items suggested a likely date in the early seventh century AD. The tomb also revealed an odd mix of Christian and pagan influences which pointed to a period when the kingdom was in the process of conversion. Britain's leading expert on the Anglo-Saxons, H. M. Chadwick, visited the site in August 1939 and immediately identified it as belonging to Raedwald, who died around 625, and is known from Bede's account to have been ambivalent about Christianity. This identification has been generally accepted ever since, although the site's most recent excavator, Professor Carver, has pointed out that there is no definite proof that the body in Mound One was Raedwald, or even a king at all as we understand the term.

If it was Raedwald, he was not a big man physically: the remnant of one of his leather shoes has been measured as a British size seven (Carver). But whoever he was, he provides by far the best surviving example of the equipment of an English warlord of the early seventh century. Perhaps his near-contemporaries in land-locked Mercia would not have had access to some of his more exotic possessions, nor have been buried with a ship, but if we want to imagine how Penda, or even Offa, would have looked when they fought at the head of their armies, the image of the 'Sutton Hoo Man' is as close as we can get.

At the time of the discovery the legal position of the finds was complicated. Basically, a coroner's court had to decide whether any coins or other precious metals which were excavated had been buried permanently, or whether those who had concealed them intended to retrieve them later. In the latter case the treasure belonged to the Crown, probably because the presumption was that they had been hidden for the purpose of evading taxes (Carver). On the other hand, if the hoard was intended to remain in the ground, it was the property of the landowner. The Suffolk coroner was convinced by the argument that there had once been a body in Mound One, and that the items had been interred as grave goods. Mrs Pretty therefore became the owner of this enormously valuable treasure, which she generously donated to the British Museum, where it is now on display.

The 'Staffordshire Hoard'

Until 2009 the finds from Sutton Hoo were unrivalled as the iconic example of Anglo-Saxon military splendour. What has since become known as the Staffordshire Hoard was in some ways even more spectacular, and certainly more unexpected. It was unearthed in south Staffordshire in July 2009 by Terry Herbert, an experienced member of the metal-detecting fraternity. Professional archaeologists are often unhappy about the idea of amateurs roaming the country-side with metal detectors, and some users have in the past given the hobby a bad name. Valuable sites have been disturbed, finds of historical interest have been sold secretly before archaeologists have had a chance to study them, and some of those that have come to the notice of the profession have been hastily dug up by untrained people, so that important information about their context has been lost. On the other hand there is now a lot of material available for study, especially small coin finds, which, without the metal detectors, would probably never have come to light.

Mr Herbert's response to his discovery was exemplary, and must surely help to improve the reputation of the hobby among the professionals as well as setting an example to its practitioners. It helped that he was acting entirely legally, as he had written permission for his investigations from the farmer who owned the field. He immediately informed the finds liaison officer for Staffordshire, who organised an excavation with the aid of the museums in Birmingham and Stoke-on-Trent. It was not long before the extraordinary nature of Mr Herbert's discovery became apparent, and by September portions of the hoard were on view at Birmingham Museum and Art Gallery. The West Midlands is not a region with a wealth of spectacular archaeological sites, and perhaps for this reason the find caught the imagination of the public in a city whose history is all too often perceived as beginning with the Industrial Revolution. Enormous queues formed in all weathers to see the exhibits, the museum had to extend its opening hours to cope, and a successful campaign was launched to raise the money needed to compensate the finders and keep the hoard in the Midlands. The towns of Stafford, Walsall, Lichfield and Tamworth, as well as Birmingham, all put in claims to display the treasure, in most cases based on its supposed connection with local celebrities such as Offa (see, for example, the *Tamworth Herald* of 20 January 2011, 'Mercian Gold Comes Home'). In the meantime it was taken to London to be investigated and restored at the British Museum. At the time of writing a selection of items is on show at the Birmingham Museum and Art Gallery, which, together with a site in Stafford, will be the hoard's eventual home.

The Treasure Act of 1996 no longer takes into account the motivation of the people who originally buried the items, which is perhaps fortunate, because a coroner would find little evidence on which to base a ruling about the intentions of whoever concealed this hoard. It is highly unusual in a number of ways. The site where it was found is on high ground south-west of Lichfield, on the edge of what in Anglo-Saxon times would have been a belt of hilly and heath-covered country running from Cannock Chase to the Birmingham Plateau. The immediate area has been farmed since the later Middle Ages, but there seem to be no Anglo-Saxon burial sites or other signs of occupation, and it was described in Domesday Book as 'waste'. The obvious inference is that whoever buried the treasure in such a spot intended to hide it, not so much from Vikings or other marauders as from the inhabitants of the Trent Valley below.

The composition of the hoard is unlike anything found elsewhere. Bags or chests of gold and silver coins were sometimes hidden near settlements for safekeeping, especially in the Viking era, and before their conversion to Christianity the English were in the habit of burying extensive collections of grave goods – Sutton Hoo is the most spectacular example – with the bodies of their leaders. But the Staffordshire Hoard contains no coins, and in fact almost nothing at all of a civilian nature apart from the remains of four or five Christian crosses, and a few pins, buckles and similar small pieces of uncertain function which may be fastenings for armour or other military equipment. Otherwise it consists mainly of fittings from sword hilts, and pieces of at least one helmet.

The sword fittings have been prised off the weapons or their scabbards, sometimes being damaged in the process, and the crosses have been deliberately bent or folded to make them easier to carry. The bulk of the metal – including the helmet fragments – is gold or silver; in fact the total amount of gold is around five kilograms, which far exceeds any other finds in England, including at Sutton Hoo. Many of the items are decorated with garnet – probably imported from Central Europe and which must in itself have been an expensive material – which is also cut to shape and set with superb craftsmanship. Some of this work is so intricate that Birmingham Museum has deemed it necessary to display the stones under a magnifying glass in order for visitors to appreciate it. The whole collection was originally buried in a leather bag, but at some point before its discovery a plough seems to have ripped open the bag and scattered its contents across a portion of the field. One can only sympathise with the obscure ploughman who so nearly unearthed what would have been a treasure beyond his wildest dreams!

Scholars will be spending many more years studying, restoring and interpreting all this material, and it might one day be possible to explain the circumstances in which it was hidden, but in the meantime we can make some inferences which are of interest for our subject. The exact dating of the hoard is still controversial, but the style of the decorated objects points to the seventh century, with most scholars favouring the period between 650 and 700 (Leahy and Bland). Potentially the most useful item for dating purposes is a strip of gold bearing a Biblical quotation in Latin, although no definitive conclusion on it seems to have yet been reached.

The find can hardly represent grave goods, either interred where they were found or looted and reburied by grave robbers, because so many of the non-military items characteristically found in rich graves are missing. For the same reason, it is not likely to be an unsorted collection of loot hurriedly gathered up by a raiding army or stripped from the bodies of the enemy after a battle. At least some of the men who carried such richly decorated swords must surely also have worn the heavy gold buckles, for example, which are found in graves at Sutton Hoo and elsewhere. These were valuable objects, and much easier to remove from corpses than pieces which were riveted to sword hilts, but none was found with the Staffordshire Hoard.

Another consideration arguing against it being the spoils of a single raid or battle is that we have no historical record of an event which could account for it. The collection represents at the very least around eighty or ninety expensive gold- and garnet-decorated swords, weapons which seem from experience at other sites to have been restricted to the wealthiest and highest-ranking warriors. If so many of a kingdom's leading men had been slain in one battle, alongside a proportionate number of their less well-armed followers, it would represent a disaster that would surely have shaken any Anglo-Saxon kingdom to its core. Apart from the attack on the Lichfield area mentioned in the 'Marwnad Cynddylan', however, we have no record of a major battle fought in this district. In fact the period when the hoard was probably buried was one in which Mercia was in the ascendancy over its neighbours, and this core area of the kingdom was relatively untouched by warfare.

On balance the most plausible theory regarding the hoard's origin is that put forward by Professor Nicholas Brooks, who believes that kings of this period would have kept a store of presti-gious war gear for issue to warriors who joined their service, and perhaps also as a means to reward brave deeds and loyal service by their existing followers. Many of these items could have been donated by vassals as tribute or 'heriot', a kind of death duty paid by a man's heirs in exchange for permission to inherit his property. Others might well have been acquired as loot: *Beowulf* describes how, after Ongentheow's death in battle, his mail shirt, sword hilt and helmet were collected and taken to Hygelac, the victor. It seems very likely that among the treasure amassed by a successful king there would have been a selection of gold and silver pieces specifically selected for recycling into new weapons, the original blades having been discarded because they were damaged, or of inferior quality, or perhaps for superstitious reasons.

The man who amassed this hoard must then have been a successful war leader, based in Mercia, who had won numerous battles in his career – enough to have run up a score of nearly a hundred dead enemies of the highest rank. Although not a Christian – the irreverent way in which the crosses were treated suggests they were thought of only as bullion – he had obviously included Christian armies among his victims. The Biblical inscription referred to above is a quotation from the Book of Numbers, and reads, in the words of the King James translation: 'Rise up lord, and let thine enemies be scattered; and let them that hate thee flee before thee.' We can imagine it being intended as a desperate prayer (not, evidently, answered in this case) for deliverance from a heathen oppressor. There is one obvious candidate: Penda. How he came to lose this treasure can only be speculation, but it might have been stolen during the chaos following his death at the Winwaed, then buried by a thief who did not live to retrieve it. Alternatively it could have been hidden from the occupying Northumbrians in the same period, then left forgotten in its remote location when those responsible failed to return from the war which restored Mercia's independence. Whatever the route by which it came down to us, it is likely to remain the definitive evidence of the splendour of Mercia's first great king.

Chapter 6

Penda's Successors and the Rise of Offa

Although he ruled only a part of the country, Peada's short reign was of longlasting significance for Mercia as a whole, because unlike his father he was a Christian. He had either been converted by missionaries who had been operating in the country during Penda's last years or, as Bede claims, had accepted the new religion as a condition of being allowed to marry Oswy's daughter Alchfled. The first Bishop of Mercia and the Middle Angles, a Scot named Diuma, was soon installed, an abbey was founded at Peterborough, and the conversion of the people gathered pace. From this time on, the heartland of Mercia enjoyed a period of relative security, and the landscape gradually came to resemble the one familiar to us today, with permanent villages, churches and monasteries replacing the pagan temples and burial grounds.

Bede confirms the Chronicle's allegation that Peada, 'it is said', was killed in 656 through his wife's treachery. We have no further details of the murder, but it is reasonable to suspect Oswy's hand in the affair. Possibly Peada was trying to re-assert Mercian independence, and the Northumbrian king was right to be concerned. Bede tells us that three years later three Mercian noblemen named Immin, Eafa and Eadbert rose in revolt, drove out the Northumbrians, and 'boldly recovered their liberty and lands.' They do not, however, appear to have considered renouncing their new faith. They placed on the throne another Christian son of Penda, Wulfhere, whom they had kept in hiding during the Northumbrian occupation.

Wulfhere

Wulfhere is depicted by Bede as a pious young man, but he lost no time in restoring Mercia's military reputation. In fact his adoption of Christianity had immediate practical benefits, because he seems to have used it to strengthen his ties with several of the kings of south-eastern England. Around 670 he married Eormenhild, the daughter of King Eorconberht of Kent, and the Anglo-Saxon Chronicle notes that King Aethelwald of the South Saxons was his god-son. The West Saxon Cenwalh – who had been forced to take refuge in East Anglia after he had insulted Penda by abandoning his sister – had returned to Wessex, and in 661, apparently while Cenwalh was occupied by fighting in Devon, Wulfhere launched an attack in the area of Ashdown. The Anglo-Saxon Chronicle goes on to say that he subdued the Isle of Wight, then subject to the kings of Wessex, and handed it to his god-son Aethelwald.

This brief notice is all we know of what must have been an extraordinary campaign. Wulfhere had led his army right through the heart of Wessex, built or otherwise acquired a fleet, and transported his troops across the Solent before the West Saxons could react. Although the Chronicle describes him as 'raiding' the Isle of Wight, it is likely that many of the inhabitants preferred him to the rule of Wessex. Bede says that the people of Wight were not Angles or Saxons but Jutes like the men of Kent, which is unlikely to be true of most of them in an ethnic sense, but does indicate that they considered themselves distinct from the West Saxons, who had attacked them on previous occasions and were to do so again after Wulfhere's death. In 686, again according to Bede, the West Saxon king Caedwalla recaptured the island, found it still devoted to paganism, and attempted to solve the problem by exterminating the inhabitants and replacing them with West Saxon settlers. Fortunately he was unsuccessful, but the invasion finally convinced the men of Wight of the advisability of conversion, 'last of all the provinces of Britain' to adopt Christianity.

By 670 Wulfhere had established a hegemony in southern England which had eluded even Penda. Kent and Surrey were ruled respectively by his brothers-in-law Ecgberht and Frithuwold, and according to Bede the joint kings of the East Saxons, Sigehere and Saebbi, also reigned as his vassals. In 664 there had been a serious outbreak of plague and a disillusioned Sigehere had turned back to the pagan religion, rebuilding ruined temples and setting up idols in them. Wulfhere had sent Bishop Jaruman to counter the apostasy and re-established the Church, and the extent of his power is shown by Bede's statement that he then sold the see of London to Wini, a former bishop of the West Saxons. Wulfhere was therefore the first Mercian king to control London, even though he still did so indirectly through his East Saxon subordinates. The post-Roman history of the city up till this time remains obscure, and it is still sometimes argued that the site was at one point entirely deserted, though Bede's statement that 'the people of London' expelled their bishop, Mellitus, in 616 makes it clear that it was thriving again by the beginning of the seventh century. It was commonly referred to as 'Lundenwic', the 'wic' element indicating a trading post, and it may always have been inhabited mainly by Frisians and other foreign merchants, but it was by far the wealthiest place in Mercia's sphere of influence, and its submission was a considerable coup for Wulfhere. Its only rivals as centres of trade were Southampton, under West Saxon control, and Ipswich in East Anglia. Mercia was no longer a barbarous frontier region, but a developing kingdom fit to take its place among the Christian states of Europe.

Further north Wulfhere seems also to have brought Lindsey into his orbit – when the see of Lichfield was founded in 669 the Christians of Lindsey were placed under its authority. The expansion of Mercian power in the south was greatly aided by the maintenance of peace with the old enemy, Northumbria. Oswy remained on good terms with Wulfhere, and consequently in 670 succeeded in being the first Northumbrian king on record to die in his bed.

Around this time the town of Lichfield began its rise to prominence as the religious centre of Mercia. On the death of Jaruman in 667, Wulfhere asked Archbishop Theodore for a replacement. The choice fell on a certain Chad, who had already been consecrated, but was currently living in a Northumbrian monastery. He rode south –

he preferred to walk but Theodore ordered him to ride a horse as more appropriate to his rank – and established a headquarters in what Bede calls 'the town of Lyccidfelth'. Despite this description there are few if any archaeological signs that there was a town there at all before Chad's arrival, but he built a church and a house, probably situated near the site of Saint Chad's Well at Stowe, half a mile north of the present cathedral, and a settlement began to grow up around it.

Towards the end of Wulfhere's reign, however, the entente with Northumbria collapsed. Oswy's successor, Ecgfrith, was less well disposed towards his southern neighbour, and seems to have been scheming to regain control of Lindsey. According to Eddius Stephanus, an eighth-century Northumbrian source, in 674 Wulfhere 'stirred up all the southern nations' and marched against Ecgfrith with the aim of enslaving his people. They met in battle at an unknown location, where after 'countless' warriors had fallen on both sides, the Mercians were routed. Bede says that Ecgfrith then annexed Lindsey, and in the aftermath of his shock defeat the new king of Wessex, Aescwine, also declared war on Wulfhere. The Mercians and West Saxons fought at Biedanheafod or Beda's Head, another unidentified site, in 675. The Anglo-Saxon Chronicle does not record the outcome, though Henry of Huntingdon says that the Mercians had the better of a hard-fought encounter in which 'many thousands' were killed on each side. But within a year both the opposing kings were dead – in Wulfhere's case, says Henry, not in battle but from disease.

Aethelred and Victory in the North

The throne passed to Aethelred, whose twenty-nine-year reign consolidated the gains made by his predecessors and left behind a relatively stable and secure northern frontier. Opinions on his character differ widely. To William of Malmesbury he was 'more famed for his pious disposition than his skill in war', but Bede would probably have disagreed. He recounts how in 676 Aethelred led an army into Kent, which had been threatening the Mercian satellite kingdoms of Essex and Surrey. He ravaged the country with his 'wicked soldiery', looting and destroying monasteries and churches, and damaging the town of Rochester so severely that Bishop Putta despaired of restoring it and went into retirement instead. This brutality had its desired effect, because the Kentish kings Hlothere and Eadric submitted to Aethelred and the threat in the south-east was removed.

In 679 the opportunity arose to avenge Wulfhere's defeat at Northumbrian hands. On this occasion King Ecgfrith had presumably invaded Mercian territory, because Aethelred confronted him on a field of which we are told only that it was 'beside the River Trent'. As usual we have few details of the encounter, except that the Mercians were victorious, and that Ecgfrith's brother Aelfwine, a young man of about 18, was killed in the battle. Aelfwine was also Aethelred's brother-in-law and, says Bede, was 'much loved' by the people of both kingdoms. His death threatened to cause a blood feud which might have led to lasting hatred between the two peoples, but Archbishop Theodore of Canterbury stepped in and negotiated a peace. The agreement held, and the Northumbrians relinquished their claim to Lindsey and never again tried to extend their power south of the Humber. For this reason Stenton has described the battle as 'one of the decisive incidents in early English history'.

Ecgfrith turned his attention instead to conquests in Scotland and Ireland, where Bede says that he and his commanders 'wretchedly abused and burned God's churches', so that the Irish, who had until then been friendly to the English, prayed to heaven for vengeance. They got it in May 685 when the Northumbrians suffered a second catastrophe at Nechtansmere, near Dunnichen in Angus. Ecgfrith was killed, along with most of his army, by the Picts under Bridei mac Beli. Henry of Huntingdon says that Ecgfrith was lured into difficult terrain by a feigned retreat and then surrounded. This battle, as much as Aethelred's victory on the Trent, ensured that Northumbria could never again aspire to dominate the whole of Britain.

In the south Caedwalla of Wessex fought a series of campaigns in Kent in the 690s, apparently without any interference from Aethelred.

In one of these campaigns Caedwalla's brother Mul was killed, and in 694 Caedwalla's successor Ine again invaded Kent and imposed a heavy fine for the killing. It is not clear why this did not lead to war between Wessex and Mercia, but the remainder of Aethelred's reign passed fairly peacefully, marred only by the murder of his wife, Queen Osthryth, in 696. Osthryth was the sister of Ecgfrith of Northumbria, and some scholars have postulated that she was involved in a Northumbrian plot to overthrow her husband. On the other hand her family had killed countless Mercians over the years, and she may have been the victim of a blood feud that had simmered secretly despite Archbishop Theodore's intervention. We do not hear that Aethelred punished anyone for the crime, but neither is there any suspicion that he was guilty himself. He abdicated in 704 and became abbot of the monastery at Bardney in Lindsey, where both his wife and her uncle King Oswald were buried.

Coenred and Ceolred

Wulfhere's son Coenred took the throne on Aethelred's retirement, but ruled for only five years. Felix's *Life of Saint Guthlac* records that during this time the Welsh were active in raiding the western provinces of the country, inflicting 'pillage and devastation', and fighting 'many skirmishes and battles' with the Mercians. Nevertheless Coenred must have defended his frontiers successfully, because charter evidence shows that he remained in control of London. In 709 he abdicated and became a monk, travelling to Rome with his friend King Offa of the East Saxons, who was also following the fashion for spiritually inclined kings to change to an ecclesiastical career.

Of the only slightly longer reign of Coenred's cousin, Ceolred, the chroniclers have little more to say. According to the Anglo-Saxon Chronicle he succeeded in 709, and six years later fought a battle against Ine of Wessex at Woden's Barrow, a famous land-mark which is believed to be the prehistoric tumulus now known as Adam's Grave, near Alton Priors in Wiltshire. A site so far south suggests a Mercian invasion of Wessex, but we know nothing of the events which led to it. In fact contemporary sources do not even tell us the outcome of the battle. Henry of Huntingdon says that 'the slaughter was so great on both sides, that it is difficult to say who sustained the severest loss,' but William of Malmesbury refers to the Mercian king as the victor.

A letter from the English missionary Saint Boniface to Ceolred's successor Aethelbald gives us the only description of this king's character, and it was not favourable. According to Boniface, Ceolred was guilty of destroying monasteries and seducing nuns, and eventually received a well-deserved punishment for his immorality. In 716, while feasting with his nobles, he was suddenly stricken by 'an evil spirit', and soon afterwards died 'raving mad, gibbering with demons and cursing the priests of God', without having had an opportunity to confess his sins and so save himself from the torments of hell. The nature of the king's illness is of course impossible to deduce from this information, and Boniface is not necessarily a reliable source on the subject, as his aim in writing this account was to frighten Aethelbald into renouncing his own sins. Ceolred was nevertheless one of the few Mercian kings in this era who remained on the throne until the end of his life and still managed to end his days peacefully. The Anglo-Saxon Chronicle tells us that he was buried at Lichfield, which suggests that he was holding court somewhere nearby when he died: perhaps Seckington or Tamworth, both places favoured by his successors, which were probably already royal residences in Ceolred's day.

Aethelbald

He was succeeded, apparently without much trouble, by Aethelbald, who was a descendant of Penda's brother Eowa and so a member of a junior branch of the royal house. That Aethelbald had a plausible claim to the throne had obviously been recognised earlier, as we learn from the *Life of Saint Guthlac* that the saint, who was also related to the Mercian royal family, had once given him shelter in his fenland retreat. This obviously relates to a period when the future king was living in exile, no doubt driven out by Ceolred as a potential rival.

surviving section of the Roman Icknield Street in Sutton Coldfield Park, approximately ten
south of its junction with Watling Street at Wall. Although the ditches on either side are
lly filled in, the original metalled surface is still visible. Such roads allowed Mercian armies to
swiftly across the country long after the departure of the legions that had built them.

Roman settlement at Wall, believed to have been a principal Mercian stronghold in the
th century. The royal hall was probably situated on the hill where the church now stands.

3. Excavated Roman ruins at W
These stood considerably high
Anglo-Saxon times, and may h
been incorporated into a defen
perimeter justifying the Welsh
description of the site as a 'cae
fortress.

4. Sculptures depicting promir
saints and kings of England
decorate the façade of Lichfiel
Cathedral, briefly the seat of a
Mercian archbishop in the eig
century.

idealised representation of Penda,
incongruously carrying a
tian cross, on the front of Lichfield
dral.

6. Offa, as depicted on the facade of
field Cathedral. The bishop's mitre
an appropriate symbol of the close
es with the church which buttressed
his power.

7. Saint Chad's Well at Stowe, near Lichfield. Largely forgotten today, was an important place pilgrimage in the Middl Ages, and may mark the spot where Chad establi his seat as bishop of Me in the late seventh centu

8. A close up view of the gold- and garnet-decorated hilt from a reproduction of the Sutton Hoo king's sword. This elaborate ornamentation is characteristic of the weapons carried by elite warriors of the seventh century, and several similar examples have been found in the Staffordshire Hoard. (*Mark Talbot*)

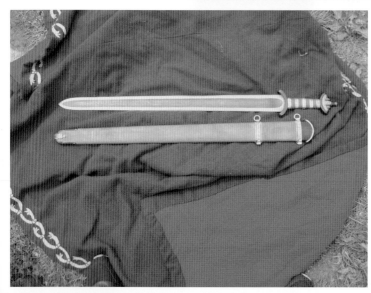

9. A reproduction Anglo- Saxon sword of around th ninth century, based on a example discovered at Gi in Yorkshire in 1976, and in the Yorkshire Museum plainer 'lobed' pommel is typical of both English an Scandinavian weapons of Viking era. (*Paul Craddock, Mercia Sveiter*)

). A reconstruction of the ghth-century Coppergate met from York. Note the nasal and hinged cheek , which together provide t complete protection for e without compromising wearer's vision. Like the n Hoo sword this was an nsive item, typical of the ra when warfare was the erve of a privileged elite. (*Paul Craddock, Mercia Sveiter*)

11. Another view of the reconstructed Coppergate helmet, showing the reinforcing bars across the crown and the mail aventail to protect the neck. (*Paul Craddock, Mercia Sveiter*)

12. A reproduction ngenhelm, a simpler and er type of helmet popular with Frankish and Viking ors in the ninth and tenth centuries. Although no examples have yet been xcavated in England, it is that similar helmets were espread in Mercia during Viking Wars. (*Mercia Sveiter*)

13. The church of All Saints at Brix[...] Northamptonshire. Probably built [...] the reign of Offa, this is the largest [...] best-preserved building of the Ang[...] Saxon period in England. Stone quarrying and brick making appea[...] have been lost arts in Offa's day, a[...] church is constructed mainly from [...] materials plundered from the ruins [...] Roman Leicester.

14. The tower at Brixworth. Solidly [...] and with narrow windows suitable [...] archers to shoot from, the smaller r[...] tower seems perfectly designed for [...] defence. However, it is not certain [...] was constructed at the same time a[...] original church, and it may have be[...] added in the ninth or tenth century [...] response to the Viking threat.

15. The River Tame at [Tam]worth. Offa's capital was [sit]ed at the junction of the [T]ame and Anker, but we [ha]ve no evidence that they [were im]portant for navigation.

Although the modern [w]atercourse seems quite [adequ]ate for Viking longships [o]r English equivalents, it [m]ay have been shallower, [slow-]flowing and less reliable [in th]e days before the banks [were] artificially straightened.

16. Tamworth Castle. Built by the Normans in a strategic location overlooking the confluence of the two rivers, it is possible that it occupies the site where Offa's hall had stood three centuries earlier, explaining why no trace of the latter has been found. Alternatively the lost hall may lie beneath the church of Saint Editha, a short distance to the north.

[Th]e River Ouse at Bedford. [Some]where on this stretch of [r]iver the lost mausoleum [of K]ing Offa may still await [ ] future archaeologists.

18. In many places part series of earthworks kn Offa's Dyke are still eas visible on the ground. T section is near Craignar north of Oswestry, on t border between Mercia the Welsh kingdom of F

19. In this sector the eastern slope of the dyke is relatively gentle, supporting the theory that its intention was to deter incursions from the west.

20. The steep approach top of Offa's Dyke from western side, facing the Berwyn Mountains. The not a serious obstacle to lightly equipped Welsh unless defended by a substantial garrison, it v have been clear of trees first built and must hav an imposing sight, visib many miles.

Aethelbald had inherited a powerful kingdom, thanks to the efforts of his predecessors, but was soon to take it to new heights. He was fortunate in that his main rival, Ine of Wessex, was distracted by internal troubles, and in 726 abdicated and retired to Rome, where he died. Bede completed his *History* in the year 731, and his final chapter, describing the 'present state of Britain', provides a useful snapshot of the political situation in the middle of Aethelbald's reign. After listing the bishops of Kent, the East, West and South Saxons, the Mercians, the Hwicce, Lindsey, the Isle of Wight, and 'the folk who live in the west, beyond the River Severn', Bede adds that 'all these provinces', and all the others south of the River Humber, were 'subject to Aethelbald, king of the Mercians'. Northumbria remained outside the Mercian sphere of influence, but the two great English kingdoms were then at peace, to the extent that many Northumbrians had renounced the life of the warrior in favour of monastic vows. The Picts and Scots were also quiet, says Bede, and although the 'Britons' of Wales and the west continued to hate the English, they had been at least partially subdued and were for the time being powerless to harm them.

The peace was not to last. In 733 Aethelbald descended on the West Saxon royal manor of Somerton in Somerset and captured it, bringing a large area of western Wessex under his direct control. Four years later he led an apparently unprovoked raid on Northumbria, 'despising holiness, and setting might above right', in the words of Henry of Huntingdon. Then in 740, according to the Anglo-Saxon Chronicle, the new king of Wessex, Cuthred, abandoned his allegiance and 'boldly made war' against Aethelbald. However bold his initiative, he was obviously unsuccessful, and saw the error of his ways in time to avoid drastic retribution, for three years later he was fighting alongside the Mercians against the Welsh. Henry of Huntingdon describes how in the ensuing battle the Britons deployed in 'immense multitudes' to stop the English invaders, but 'falling on the enemy's ranks at different points, in a sort of rivalry and contest which should be foremost', the allies routed them and returned home in triumph.

95

In 746 King Selred of the East Saxons was killed; the Chronicle does not say by whom, but he had also been a vassal of Aethelbald and may have perished in another unsuccessful revolt. Cuthred seems to have been distracted for the next few years by internal troubles, because the Chronicle says that in 748 'Cynric, aetheling [i.e. a royal prince] of Wessex, was killed,' perhaps in a failed bid for the throne, and in 750 Cuthred was fighting against an 'arrogant ealdorman' named Aethelhun. But in the same year the continuator of Bede tells us that the West Saxon king, his home front now no doubt secured, once more rose in revolt against Aethelbald. The phrasing of this entry hints that Cuthred was involved in much greater matters than a purely local rebellion, for it actually states that he 'rose up against King Aethelbald and Oengus.' Oengus mac Fergus was the king of the Picts, and at that time he exercised a hegemony in the north of Britain similar to that of Aethelbald in the south. In 741 he also took over the throne of the Dal Riata Scots who were settled in what is now Argyll, and became involved in conflict with both the Northumbrians and the Britons of Strathclyde, described in the twelfth-century chronicle of Simeon of Durham.

The year 750 saw the defeat of the Picts by Tewdwr of Strathclyde at the Battle of Mugdock, where Oengus' brother Talorcan, commanding the Pictish army, was killed. Six years later, however, the Picts returned in alliance with the Northumbrians, and forced Tewdwr's son and successor Domnagual to submit to them. We have no details of the role played by Mercia in this northern war, but it is not unlikely that Aethelbald had been in communication with Oengus, perhaps with a view to keeping the Northumbrians occupied in case they decided to join the British side in the 750 campaign. In that case Wessex might have been persuaded to take advantage of the fact that the Mercians were temporarily focused on their northern frontier.

In 752, according to the Anglo-Saxon Chronicle, Aethelbald and Cuthred met in battle at a place called Beorhford, which is generally identified with Burford on the River Windrush, on the slopes of the Cotswold Hills between Oxford and Circencester. Henry of Huntingdon's dramatic account relates that Aethelbald, as 'king of kings', was accompanied by allied contingents from Kent, the East Saxons and the 'Angles' (probably those of East Anglia). Fighting alongside Cuthred was the former rebel Aethelhun, now reconciled, who was entrusted with the golden dragon standard of Wessex. Before the opposing lines clashed, Aethelhun, no doubt eager to prove his loyalty, rushed forward and 'transfixed' his opposite number, who was carrying the Mercian standard. A terrible battle then took place, with the usual carnage on both sides. Aethelbald and Aethelhun both fought like heroes, mowing down their respective enemies so that the armies seemed caught between two consuming fires. 'Wherever the brave King Aethelbald turned, the enemy was slaughtered, for his invincible sword rent armour as if it were a vestment, and bones as if they were flesh.' At last the moment came when the two champions faced each other in single combat. But at the first exchange of blows Aethelbald's courage failed. Henry explains that God had decided to punish him for his pride and afflicted him suddenly with terror, so that he fled from the field even while the rest of his army was still fighting, leaving it to scatter in ignominious defeat.

Unfortunately, this exciting story is unlikely on several grounds. Henry could offer no rational motive for Aethelbald's uncharacteristic cowardice, hence his reliance on divine intervention. The pro-West Saxon Chronicle, which would have been expected to mention such a humiliation for the Mercian enemy, is silent on the matter. Not only is it out of character, but Aethelbald's behaviour seems to have had none of the expected repercussions. It is hardly likely that a war leader who suddenly abandoned his men in the presence of the enemy could retain their loyalty and respect, but Aethelbald returned to Mercia still fully in control, and there is no record that his followers turned against him until the confused events of 757, which are discussed below. It is of course quite possible that he was coming off worst in single combat when he was rescued by his bodyguards – an incident of that sort might have been gleefully remembered in Wessex without having much impact on his reputation at home.

The mention of the dragon standard may, however, reflect a genuine tradition, because William Camden says that in his day, in the late sixteenth century, the inhabitants of Burford still celebrated the battle by parading a golden dragon about the village on midsummer eve. The Chronicle is of course a West Saxon source, and may have exaggerated the extent of the victory. In fact Aethelbald's army probably withdrew more or less intact, because no deaths of eminent men are recorded apart from the standard bearer, and there seem to have been no serious consequences for Mercian power.

Cuthred went on to campaign against the Welsh, but died two years later. One of his relatives, Sigeberht, succeeded him briefly, but reigned for only a year before Cynewulf and the leading men of the kingdom deposed him for unspecified 'unlawful actions'. One of the first acts of Cynewulf, who succeeded him, must have been to visit Aethelbald's court to make his submission, because his name and those of several of his prominent followers appear as witnesses on a charter of 757 in which the Mercian made a grant of land in Wiltshire to a local abbot. That a Mercian ruler could give away land in the heart of Wessex while a young and vigorous West Saxon king stood meekly by and endorsed it says a great deal about the balance of power at the end of Aethelbald's reign, even after the apparent defeat at Beorhford.

The reputation for tyranny which Aethelbald later earned seems to have been a result of his difficulties with the church. In fact several examples of his interest in religion are recorded. Felix's account of Guthlac's life tells us that the king repaid the benefactor of his early years by commissioning building work to dignify his last resting place at Crowland, which became a place of pilgrimage. In 747, at Boniface's instigation, Aethelbald joined with Archbishop Cuthbert of Canterbury to convene a council to discuss church reform. But the king's private life, like that of his predecessor, attracted Boniface's disapproval. The letter quoted above which relates the fate of Ceolred, probably written around the time of this council, congratulates Aethelbald on his just government, his generosity to the poor and his maintenance of the rule of law in the kingdom – but it goes on to accuse the king of a list of sins very similar to those of his predecessor. He had supposedly ignored the privileges of the church, plundered monasteries and allowed his noblemen to use violence against members of the clergy. What was worse, it had been brought to Boniface's attention that Aethelbald had never married, but far from remaining single 'for the sake of chastity and continence', was in the habit of fornicating with nuns and virgins as well as with ordinary 'harlots'. Many commentators have allowed this criticism to overshadow Aethelbald's undoubted achievements, acknowledged even by Boniface himself, but they are perhaps the sort of thing which we might expect from a leader of a church which was still trying to assert itself as a political force, a reminder that the difficulties which Henry II experienced with Thomas Becket, for example, were nothing new.

Already in the eighth century the steady drift of valuable tribute-paying lands from secular to religious hands was posing a problem for the state. The church unashamedly operated a kind of moral blackmail, persuading kings and magnates to give grants of land to religious houses for the good of their souls or those of their people, while steadfastly opposing any transfers in the opposite direction. Any attempt by the king to collect revenues or military or labour service from church lands was liable to be characterised as theft of God's property and attract thinly veiled accusations of paganism, so the long-term effect was a slow but virtually irreversible decline in the resources available to the state. Even far-sighted churchmen recognised that there was a problem; Bede, in a letter to Bishop Egbert of York, argued that many people were entering monasteries in order to evade taxes or other civil obligations, and that the houses which gave them refuge were no use to God or man, and ought to be suppressed. And yet any king who tried to take action risked being anathematised by Bede's more uncompromising colleagues as an irreligious plunderer. Boniface's motive for his verdict on Aethelbald need not have been as overtly cynical as this analysis suggests, but it seems to have had the right effect. In 749, at Gumley in Leicester-shire, the king put his name to a charter which exempted the churches in his kingdom from all taxes and labour services, except for the essential maintenance of bridges and forts (Stenton).

No criticism of the king's behaviour would be likely to have much effect, though, if it had not had some basis in truth. The ageing statesman who compensates for the approaching decline of his powers by indulging in risky sexual adventures is a not unfamiliar figure today, and towards the end of his long reign Aethelbald might well have succumbed to the same sort of temptation. This may even have been a factor in his unusual end, although none of our sources gives much detail. Under the year 757 the Anglo-Saxon Chronicle records in its usual laconic style that 'Aethelbald, king of the Mercians, was killed at Seckington, and his body rests at Repton, and he reigned forty one years.' Seckington, five miles north of Tamworth, was a royal estate in the heart of Mercia, where the king might have expected to be reasonably safe. The continuation of Bede, however, adds that he was murdered one night, 'treacherously and miserably', by his own bodyguards. Stenton refers in this connection to a later document which states that Aethelbald gave lands to the abbey at Gloucester because he had attacked a kinsman of the abbess, and suggests that the king may have come to be seen as a violent oppressor.

If he had really deserted his men on the field at Beorhford this might have provided his assailants with another motive, although as we shall see, Henry of Huntingdon, our only source for this allegation, himself undermines this argument. It is of course also possible to construct lurid theories involving a predatory old tyrant and the female relatives of his retainers, but there is another curious circumstance which deserves to be taken into account. The Anglo-Saxon Chronicle for the same year includes a much longer and more detailed passage describing the death of King Cynewulf of the West Saxons, which actually occurred twenty-nine years later, but was presumably inserted here in error by a later copyist confused by the fact that 757 was the year of Cynewulf's accession. He had taken the throne of Wessex after driving out the unpopular Sigeberht, and in 786 was planning to exile Sigeberht's brother Cyneheard, no doubt as a precaution against a possible coup. Cyneheard, however, got wind of the plot and surprised the king one night at a place called Merton, where the king was 'in the company of a woman' and protected only by a small bodyguard. Cynewulf and all his thegns were killed, but an ealdorman named Osric arrived soon afterwards with a loyalist army and Cyneheard and his men were slaughtered in their turn.

The continuator of Bede seems to be just as confused as the Chronicle at this point, and wrongly states that Cynewulf 'died' in the same year as Aethelbald. In view of this coincidence the same source's statement that it was the latter who was murdered at night by his own men can hardly be regarded as reliable evidence. As this is the only source for the circumstances of Aethelbald's death, the case against his bodyguards can only be regarded as unproven. Strangely, the Peterborough version of the Anglo-Saxon Chronicle records yet another royal assassination under the same year, 757 (ascribed by the continuator of Bede to 758). King Eadberht of Northumbria had abdicated in favour of his son Oswulf, who ruled for only a year before 'his household killed him'. So unless we postulate a sudden brief epidemic of treachery among royal body-guards all over England, we must suspect that one or more of these reported incidents is the result of a chronicler's error.

In this connection Henry of Huntingdon's account is of particular interest. He says that Aethelbald was killed in an otherwise un-known battle at a place which he calls 'Secandune', presumably Seckington. The king, 'disdaining to flee' although 'the carnage was wonderful', allegedly died fighting, which implies that he had recovered from his failure of nerve at Beorhford and that his bodyguards, far from betraying their lord, were slaughtered with him. Admittedly Henry is usually disregarded as an unreliable late writer, but in this case his departure from the continuator's dubious version tends to strengthen the theory that he had an independent source. It is of course possible that both versions contain a grain of truth, and that the Battle of Secandune or Seckington, if it ever took place, was the result of a civil war between factions at the Mercian court. Certainly if an army from a hostile kingdom had penetrated so far into Mercia we might have expected the Anglo-Saxon Chronicle to take note of it. Nevertheless, rather than seeing Aethelbald as a tyrant whose cruelties and sexual conduct provoked his own followers into revolt, we may be justified in quoting as his epitaph a less-remembered passage from Boniface's famous letter: 'peace is established in your kingdom. For this we rejoice and praise God.'

Who did kill Aethelbald, and why, we will never know. The Anglo-Saxon Chronicle says that one Beornred replaced him on the throne of Mercia 'and held it a little while, and unhappily.' Whether he was a legitimate successor or a usurper who had overthrown his master by treachery, it was Beornred's misfortune to find himself opposed by one of the most formidable characters in the whole of English history. He clearly put up a fight, but his reign can have lasted no more than a few months. In the entry for the year of Aethelbald's death, the continuator of Bede concludes with the statement that 'Offa, having put Beornred to flight, sought to gain the kingdom by bloodshed.' From this we can deduce that Beornred and Offa were not the only contenders for the throne, but that none of the latter's rivals lasted long enough to be credited with the kingship.

Whether the 'bloodshed' involved pitched battles, a purge of those suspected of Aethelbald's murder, or merely the hunting down and killing of fugitive pretenders to the throne, we do not know. Writing much later, Matthew of Westminster says that the people, 'both noble and ignoble', rebelled against Beornred because he disregarded the laws and ruled as a tyrant. Offa, 'a most gallant young man', was then accepted unanimously as their leader. He may have presented himself as Aethelbald's avenger, or he might even have been one of those who disposed of him, but in any case he must have acted swiftly and ruthlessly, and can hardly have succeeded so quickly without some popular support. By the end of the year 757 Offa was the unchallenged master of Mercia, and was to remain so for the next thirty-nine years.

Offa's Pedigree

So who was this Offa? The Anglo-Saxon Chronicle follows its usual practice with prominent rulers by breaking off its narrative to insert a long genealogy. Offa's father, we are told, was Thingfrith, son of Eanwulf, son of Osmod, son of Eowa, son of Pybba. Eowa, of course, we have encountered before: he was the brother of Penda who was killed at the Battle of Maserfelth in 642. An interesting analysis of the Mercian royal family tree suggests that there was a long-running struggle for the throne among at least three different branches of the family, who can be identified because their candidates bore names beginning with a particular letter of the alphabet (D. Dumville, in Bassett). This is not as far-fetched as it sounds, as series of alliterative names are quite common in Anglo-Saxon genealogies. Thus Offa's opponent Beornred would have belonged to a line which later came to power with kings Beornwulf, Beorhtwulf and Burgred in the ninth century.

A rival 'C' family, descended from Penda's brother Coenwealh, may also have re-emerged after Offa's death in the reign of Coenwulf (798–821). Unfortunately, however, there is no evidence apart from the names that most of these men were related to each other at all, and Offa's own genealogy shows that the tradition of alliteration was not universal. This theory therefore gives us no real insight into the realities of Mercian power politics, and the best that can be said is that Offa was related, if distantly, to both Penda and Aethelbald, and so presumably had a valid claim to the throne by the prevailing rules of succession. But there must have been plenty of other candidates with at least as good a title, so Offa's pedigree would have been of no value if he had not been able to prove himself the most fitted to rule, if necessary by force of arms.

Chapter 7

The Warrior in the Age of the Mercian Kings

Offensive Weapons

Offa's power, like that of all his contemporaries, rested ultimately on the fighting men he could command. The English soldier of the seventh and eighth centuries typically fought on foot with spear, sword and shield. Swords were expensive to make, and although the recent evidence of the Staffordshire Hoard suggests that they were more common than was once thought, it is unlikely that many men outside the professional warrior class would have been able to afford one. The weapon most closely associated with the Anglo-Saxons, and the one whose possession in effect defined a free man, was the spear. The cultural significance of the spear was enormous. Old English poetry had a dozen or so different terms for it, several alluding to the ash wood of which the shaft was traditionally made. Hence warriors could be described by titles such as 'ash-bearers'. It is even possible that the name of the Angles themselves derived from the same root as 'angon', a Frankish term for a throwing spear. Most of our evidence for Anglo-Saxon spears comes from graves of the pagan era, in which men were frequently, though by no means always, buried with weapons (Swanton, 1973). About 85 per cent of the weapon finds in these graves are of spearheads, though this does not necessarily reflect their predominance in actual warfare. Because of their symbolic importance, and no doubt their relative cheapness, which would make them less likely to be coveted by

104

surviving relatives, spears might have been particularly favoured as burial objects even for men who also possessed other weapons. Even boys far too young to fight were sometimes buried with them.

The famous 'Franks casket', a whalebone box carved in unmistakeable English style and probably dating from around the eighth century, provides some of the earliest pictorial evidence for Anglo-Saxon warriors of the period. It is decorated with scenes from the Bible and Classical history as well as Germanic legend, but the models for the figures were no doubt those of the artist's own day. The runic inscriptions are characteristic of Anglian rather than Saxon dialects, which place its origin somewhere in northern or central England. Discovered in France but now in the British Museum, it is usually thought to be of Northumbrian origin, but could equally well be Mercian. Most of the warriors depicted are carrying spears, and the same applies to a group of men shown watching Romulus and Remus being suckled by a wolf, who lack shields or armour and are thought to represent shepherds (Swanton, 1998). Professor Swanton remarks that shepherds 'would have been wise to carry a spear', and the casket may reflect a time when any man whose work took him into isolated places would have routinely gone armed. Early Anglo-Saxon countrymen may have found a spear a valuable multi-functional item, as some African tribesmen still do today. Apart from defending livestock against wolves, it would have been useful against rustlers or those who sought to pursue a blood feud by taking members of a rival community unawares. And unlike a sword, a spear can also double as a walking stick or a support to lean on during long hours of guard duty.

Archaeologists have identified as many as forty different designs of iron spearhead (Swanton, 1973), but most of these are probably attributable to local variations in manufacturing techniques, or even the idiosyncrasies of individual smiths. The most common type was roughly lozenge shaped, fairly long (between twelve and eighteen inches) and heavy, with a sharply pointed blade, and seems to have been designed for thrusting rather than throwing. Swanton suggested that excavated examples show a detectable increase in size and strength as time went on, but the practice of burying weapons in graves gradually died out after the conversion of the country to Christianity, so we have very little evidence from after the mid-seventh century. One variant had projecting metal 'wings' fixed to the socket below the blade, which are usually interpreted as designed to stop the spear penetrating too far into a victim's body.

Although this type is common in illustrations from the later Anglo-Saxon period (including on the Bayeux tapestry), it is very rare in graves, suggesting that it did not become widespread until the Christian era. An important question which cannot easily be resolved by archaeology is the length of the shafts, as the wood itself is seldom preserved. Some graves contain both a spearhead and an iron ferrule which would presumably have been fitted to the other end of the shaft, and from the positions of these items it has been estimated that the shafts varied between about five and a half and eight feet in length (Underwood). This is not necessarily conclusive evidence, however, as they may have been shortened, or shorter versions selected, in order to fit conveniently into the graves. Actual shafts from the third or fourth centuries AD, found preserved in a bog at Nydam in Denmark, were slightly longer. It is of course likely that a man would choose to use a spear of length suitable to his own height, and that shorter weapons might have been reserved for throwing, but illustrations such as the carvings on the Franks casket confirm that the typical thrusting spear was somewhat longer than the height of a man.

Another group of spearheads seems to have belonged to specialised missile weapons, which might be better described as javelins. These are much smaller, and often barbed. Particularly interesting are those with a long, thin metal shank like the Roman 'pilum' or the Frankish 'angon', which was designed to bend when the head stuck in an opponent's shield. We have no contemporary accounts of their use in battle in England, but they do appear occasionally in pagan-period graves, for example at Prittlewell in Essex (Underwood). The Byzantine writer Agathias described the effects of the angon in Frankish hands at the Battle of Casilinum in 554. A man whose shield had been struck and penetrated could not pull the spear out because of the barbs, nor could he easily cut the iron shaft to

106

release it, so was forced to carry the unwieldy object around with him, dragging on the ground and making it hard to manoeuvre his shield. 'When the Frank sees this he quickly treads on it with his foot, stepping on the ferrule and forcing his shield downwards so that the man's grip is loosened and his head and breast bared. Then, taking him unprotected, he kills him easily.'

An additional advantage of this type of weapon was that once the shaft was bent it could not be thrown back by an enemy even if he did succeed in extracting it from the shield. Why such an effective design was eventually abandoned is not clear, as it would seem to be the ideal counter to the defensive use of shields. Again, the problem may simply be the shortage of archaeological evidence in the Christian period. At the Battle of Maldon Byrhtnoth is said to have thrown a spear which burst his victim's coat of mail and wounded him fatally in the heart, which is the kind of effect that would be expected from a heavy spear with a sharply pointed tip like an angon. It may, however, have been considered more cost effective to concentrate on general-purpose designs suitable for both throwing and stabbing, and there seems no reason why the large-headed thrusting types could not have been thrown over short distances in emergencies.

Approximately one pagan grave in six contains the remains of a sword or swords, although as discussed above this is hardly conclusive evidence for their frequency in life. Hilts often incorporated materials such as gold and garnet, which survive in the ground while iron rusts away, and their decoration shows more variation over time than do the associated blades, so most archaeological attention has focused on the development of the hilts and other fittings. From a purely practical point of view the design of sword blades changed very little during the Anglo-Saxon period. It did not need to change, as it had already reached a high level of sophistication by the fourth or fifth century AD.

The sword remained in essence the single-handed, double-edged cutting weapon of the Germanic migration period, with a blade measuring between twenty-eight and thirty-four inches in length. It had probably been derived from the Roman 'spatha', which was

107

originally a cavalry weapon but had gradually been adopted by footsoldiers – including Germans – serving in the armies of the later Empire. Various methods of forging the blades were in use, but the most expensive and prestigious is what is known today as 'pattern welding'. In this process any flaws or impurities in the metal are evened out by repeatedly twisting and welding together a number of iron bars, then hammering them flat. The result is a tough but flexible blade with an intricate and beautiful surface pattern some-times known as 'brogdenmael', or 'weaving marks', analogous to the appearance of woven cloth. This process was probably invented under the Roman Empire, and it became increasingly popular from the fifth century onwards. It appears to have gradually declined in the eighth century, perhaps because the availability of better-quality iron and more advanced forging techniques made it un-necessary, although as in the case of spearheads the shortage of examples in datable graves makes this trend difficult to establish. It has been suggested that the purpose of pattern welding was mainly decorative in any case, especially as it was sometimes used for items such as knives and spearheads which would hardly justify such a labour-intensive method of manufacture (Pollington).

In practice pattern-welded swords may not have been greatly superior to less sophisticated versions, as the process can make them brittle. But perhaps appearance and function were not easily separated in the minds of potential purchasers: the distinctive appearance of the blade might have served not only as a status symbol but as a sort of quality mark, indicating both to the owner and others the effort and expense which had gone into making it. Good quality swords could be fabulously expensive; one mentioned in the tenth-century will of Earl Aelfgar of Essex, for example, was valued at 120 'mancuses' of gold, or roughly the equivalent of the same number of good plough oxen.

Swords were clearly optimised for cutting or slashing rather than for thrusting. The typical blade of the pre-Viking era was parallel sided for most of its length and had a rounded rather than an acutely pointed tip, though as it was sharpened on both sides it would still be effective for stabbing, at least against an unarmoured target. Perhaps a more important consideration was that Anglo-Saxon pommels, both the decorative gold and garnet designs of the nobles' expensive weapons and the cheaper, more functional types, were too light to act as counterweights as they did on later medieval swords. This would have made the weapons somewhat blade heavy, and so perhaps more suited to deliberate, powerful cuts than to rapid manoeuvring. This may remind us of the remarks of the eleventh-century Danish writer Saxo Grammaticus, who says that 'in days of old' men did not try to beat each other down in a sword fight with a rain of blows, but relied on the force rather than the frequency of their strokes. However, Saxo was referring specifically to a rather ritualised form of single combat, and it is unlikely that men in the heat of battle would have had the time to prepare their blows carefully in this way. More probably what to modern eyes seem unbalanced Anglo-Saxon swords simply required a stronger sword arm to wield, rewarding the practice needed to master them with the ability to deliver cuts of devastating force.

Another weapon commonly associated with the Anglo-Saxons is the knife or 'seax', which is generally believed to have given the Saxons their name. Most of the seaxes found in England, however, have blades of fourteen inches or less, and look like general-purpose knives rather than weapons of war. Early types had single-edged but symmetrical blades with rounded tips, but by the sixth century a variant appeared with a sharply angled back, or even a reverse-curved tip like a Bowie knife. If the tip was sharpened on both sides in the manner of a modern Bowie knife this would have made the seax a more effective stabbing weapon, but such short blades can only have been used in combat as a last resort by a man who had lost his spear or sword. In the eighth century seaxes began to appear which were of similar design but much longer, approaching the length of short swords. Still single edged, but with relatively broad, heavy blades, these could have been very effective cutting and thrusting weapons, reminiscent of the later medieval falchion. Stephen Pollington has even suggested that some long-hilted seaxes could have been used two-handed, though he admits that this tactic is difficult to reconcile with the use of a shield.

109

Like the seax, the axe in this period was basically an agricultural or woodworking implement, with a limited application to warfare. The famous 'axe-hammer' from Sutton Hoo looks more like a tool than a weapon, perhaps connected with the maintenance of the ship it was buried with. Fifth- and sixth-century finds – for example from Burgh Castle in Norfolk – occasionally include the remains of axes with narrow curved heads which have been interpreted as belonging to throwing axes of the type used by the Franks (Underwood). The two-handed axes familiar from the Bayeux tapestry were a much later development, adopted under Scandinavian influence in the eleventh century. However, despite Henry of Huntingdon's probably anachronistic description of the West Saxon champion Aethelhun wielding one at the Battle of Beorhford in 752, there is no reliable evidence that the axe played a significant part in the wars of the Mercian era.

Apart from thrown spears, missile weapons included bows and possibly slings; the latter have left no archaeological trace, but the 'Life of Saint Wilfred' (Stephanus) describes one being used to kill a pagan priest in a passage with very obvious echoes of David and Goliath. Unfortunately archaeology can shed little more light on Anglo-Saxon archery, because the wooden bows themselves were perishable and the iron arrowheads are difficult to identify, the larger ones being easily mistaken for small spearheads.

It is often assumed, without much supporting evidence, that the early English despised the bow as a weapon of war, and that it was used mainly by the lower classes for hunting. This idea probably derives from Henry of Huntingdon, who quotes William the Conqueror as telling his men before the Battle of Hastings that the English were 'a people that does not even possess arrows'. Even for Harold's army of 1066, however, this is suspect, as a general's pep talk on the eve of a battle can hardly be taken as evidence for his enemy's real capabilities! In fact an unprejudiced investigation lends weight to the idea that the English not only used the bow in war, but used it to considerable effect. It is obvious from one of the riddles preserved in the well-known *Exeter Book* that the bow was an implement with which most people would have been familiar, and it is noteworthy that this text describes it being used against men and not as a hunting weapon.

The scene on the lid of the Franks casket shows an archer defending himself successfully from within a building against a group of assailants advancing from outside; one of them is already down with an arrow protruding from his chest, while one of his companions has two arrows in his shield and seems about to be hit in the head by another. Three other dead or wounded figures may represent further victims of the same archer, who appears to be labelled with the name 'Aegil' or 'Aegili'. Numerous attempts to identify a historical or legendary prototype for this dramatic picture have been unsuccessful, and Professor Swanton suggests that it may represent a small-scale skirmish which was of personal significance for the owner or commissioner of the box, but too commonplace to have been recorded in historical sources (Swanton, 1998). The casket is obviously an expensive item, and if Aegil the archer was its owner it shows that even high-ranking warriors did not disdain the bow. Wiglaf's eulogy for Beowulf describes his career in terms which suggest that being shot at with arrows was a typical experience in war: '... the sustainer of the warriors, who often endured the iron shower, when, string-driven, the storm of arrows sang over shield-wall.'

The poem on the Battle of Maldon is admittedly much later than our period, but there is no reason to suppose that tactics had changed significantly by the late tenth century. It contains three references to archery, including the account of the presumably high-ranking Northumbrian hostage Aescferth, who 'wavered not at the war-play, but, while he might, shot steadily from his sheaf of arrows.' In the later Middle Ages certain counties in northern and central England – Yorkshire, Lincolnshire, Nottinghamshire, Lancashire and especially Cheshire – were noted for their skilled archers, and it has been suggested that this regional specialisation might date back to Anglo-Saxon times (Bradbury). There is little real evidence for this, but if it was the case we might expect Mercian and perhaps Northumbrian armies to have made more use of the bow than their southern rivals. It is perhaps significant that the one archer who is singled out by name in *The Battle of Maldon* is a Northumbrian.

The performance of the bow has probably been subject to more misconceptions than any other aspect of medieval warfare, and the idea is still sometimes put forward that before the introduction of the 'longbow' in the thirteenth century archery was relatively ineffective. In fact there is archaeological evidence for powerful bows in England as far back as the Neolithic period. The remains found at Nydam, and an eighth-century weapon from Oberflacht in Swabia, show that early medieval bows could also be just as long and powerful as those from later centuries, and that yew, the preferred wood for longbows, was already in common use. An Anglo-Saxon-period bow from Chessel Down on the Isle of Wight was about five feet long, which is at the lower end of the size range for longbows, but bow lengths were tailored to the height of the archer and so were always highly variable (Pollington). Some authors, while conceding that Anglo-Saxon bows were not inherently weak, continue to downgrade their importance by arguing that they were drawn to the chest, and not to the chin or the ear as was customary in later centuries. This conclusion seems to be based on the figure on the Franks casket and the archers on the Bayeux tapestry, including the only example there of an Englishman with a bow, who are using very short weapons drawn rather awkwardly to their chests or stomachs. In fact this style of depicting archers was quite common throughout the Middle Ages, and was probably adopted for aesthetic reasons, so that the arrows and bowstrings would not obscure the men's faces (Strickland and Hardy). It is unwise to use it as evidence for real-life practice, which would imply that men made and used these powerful weapons in life-or-death situations for thousands of years, without ever discovering minor changes in shooting technique which would have greatly increased their effectiveness.

Defensive Equipment

A warrior's first line of defence against the weaponry arrayed against him was always his shield. As with the spear, its importance is demonstrated by its appearance in poetry, where a battle line was often described as a 'bordweall' or 'scyldburh', both terms usually translated into modern English as 'shieldwall'. The shield was circular, made of wood (traditionally linden or lime wood, although excavated remains show that many different types of wood were used in practice), and reinforced with an iron boss in the centre. It was held by a single central grip behind the boss, which served both as protection for the hand and as a weapon in its own right, capable of being punched into an opponent's face. The boss evolved over time, with seventh-century examples being taller and more pointed than earlier versions, perhaps to enhance their effectiveness in this aggressive role. There was sometimes an iron 'button' on the point of the boss which could have had the function of trapping or deflecting an enemy's weapon.

The wooden shield board itself varied in size, with some examples not much more than twelve inches across, though most were between twice and three times that in diameter. It has been claimed that English shields were originally slightly smaller than those found on the Continent, but became larger as time went on. This trend has even been used as evidence for a change in tactics, the idea being that smaller shields are better suited to individual skirmishing tactics, and bigger ones to close-formation 'shieldwall' fighting (Harke, in Hawkes). All this is highly speculative, however, as no actual shields from England survive, and estimating their dimensions from the positions of bosses and other fittings found in graves may give unrepresentative results. The shields on the Franks casket, as well as two depicted on a plaque from the Staffordshire Hoard which probably formed part of a helmet, are fairly small, probably between eighteen inches and two feet in diameter, but of course they may have been shown undersize for artistic reasons, in order not to obscure the human subjects.

The wooden part of the shield was made of a number of planks cut to shape, glued together and further strengthened with leather, which might be just a binding round the edge or, more commonly, a complete covering on the front, back or both. That the leather made an important contribution to the defensive value of a shield as well as just holding the boards together is implied by a tenth-century law of King Athelstan, which penalised men who presented themselves with shields covered in inferior sheepskin instead of the preferred cow hide. This has been confirmed by modern experiments, which showed that 'a layer of rawhide was the key to the shield being at all effective' against a sword cut (Loades). Rivets and metal plates were often added, either to strengthen the wood further or simply for decoration. Contemporary illustrations sometimes depict shields as convex in shape, a design which would provide slightly better protection for the body than a flat surface, and offer significantly greater resistance to the rippling motion of the wooden boards in response to a blow. It is usually assumed that English shields would be painted, as some Viking ones were, but this is not certain. Shields in *Beowulf* are described as yellow, but this may simply refer to a leather covering bleached by exposure to the elements. There is no evidence in this period for a system of heraldic designs which might have served to identify important men, or even for uniform shield colours or patterns within a unit, though a passage in *The Battle of Maldon* describes Earl Byrhtnoth raising his shield before making a speech, which implies that it somehow marked him out as a leader.

It is very difficult to determine how common defensive armour was in seventh- and eighth-century armies. Beowulf and his followers all wear helmets and mail coats, by which they are recognised as warriors when they arrive in Hrothgar's kingdom, but these are heroes, and their equipment, like their exploits, can be expected to be larger than life. There are only four surviving Anglo-Saxon helmets, all dated to the seventh or eighth centuries; the Staffordshire Hoard includes parts of at least another one which still awaits reconstruction, though as the excavated pieces of this item are made of gold and silver rather than iron it may have been more ceremonial than functional.

As in the case of weapons this bias towards the early part of the period may be due to the pagan habit of burying war gear in graves, though the idea that this practice ceased immediately after the conversion seems to be too simplistic. The earliest and best-known example of Anglo-Saxon headgear is the helmet from Sutton Hoo, which is generally supposed to have belonged to the early-seventh-century King Raedwald of the East Angles (see pages 80

114

to 83). The workmanship and elaborate decoration of this piece, as reconstructed by archaeologists at the British Museum, certainly befits a king, but it is by no means certain that all the other helmets belonged to men of such high rank. The four which have been reconstructed are all of different design. The Sutton Hoo specimen seems to have been inspired by Roman cavalry helmets, and consists of a one-piece metal bowl with attached neck guard, cheek pieces and full face mask. The face plate may have been more common than this single excavated example suggests, as two words used for helmets in *Beowulf*, 'grimhelm' and 'heregrima', incorporate a term meaning 'mask'.

The Benty Grange helmet, discovered in a burial mound near Buxton in Derbyshire in 1848, has been dated to the middle of the seventh century, a time and place which suggest that it may have been worn by one of the gesiths of Penda's army. It is made from plates of horn, fastened together and reinforced with iron bands, and lacks cheek pieces or a face plate, though it does have a short nasal. On the top of the helmet is a crest consisting of a bronze boar, decorated with gold and garnet and with a slot along the top to hold a strip of horsehair or similar material. These crests are also mentioned in written sources, and had a number of functions. As a symbol of the pagan gods the boar might have offered supernatural protection, but more practically it could deflect a sword cut aimed at the crown; Beowulf was said to have possessed a helmet with a crest bound with wire, which made it impossible for a sword to injure him. It is also likely that a distinctive crest would serve to identify a leader in battle. Another interesting feature of the Benty Grange helmet is a silver cross on the nasal, which despite the boar crest and the pagan style of burial implies that its owner was a Christian, and intended to be recognised as such in battle. On the other hand a member of Penda's multi-cultural army may have seen no inconsistency in wearing protective charms from as many different religions as possible.

A helmet discovered in 1997 at Wollaston in Northamptonshire also dates from around the middle of the seventh century. Like the Benty Grange example it is constructed of plates riveted to metal bands, though in this case the plates are iron, and cheek pieces were attached by hinges. It has an undecorated iron boar crest, and in general appears plain and functional, with no trace of garnet or precious-metal inlay. The latest helmet to be excavated is probably late eighth century, and was found at Coppergate in York in the 1980s. It is similar in construction to the Wollaston specimen, with the apparent addition of a mail aventail at the back, but is better made and more finely decorated.

There is abundant literary and archaeological evidence, discussed below, that blows aimed at the head were a common cause of death and injury in Anglo-Saxon battles, so we would expect head protection of some sort to have been fairly common. The shortage of archaeological remains is therefore surprising. At first glance the inventory of the Staffordshire Hoard – one helmet compared to about eighty-six sword pommels – appears to give a rough idea of the proportion of men who might wear such protection, and this is probably not inconsistent with the frequency of excavated helmets generally. However, this almost certainly overstates their rarity, and the existence of plainer varieties such as the Wollaston example suggests that they were not restricted to kings and high-ranking nobles. Helmets are mentioned several times in *Beowulf* (though usually in the context of being cut through by sword blows, which casts some doubt on the usefulness of cheaper designs). In the passage describing a surprise attack on the hall by Grendel's mother we are told that the warriors seized their swords and shields, but helmets and mail coats were ignored ('helm ne gemunde'), obviously because there was no time to put them on. *Beowulf* is a work of fiction, but it was intended to be read in just such a hall as is described here, and the implication is that the audience would expect some, if not all, of the defenders to have had helmets and armour available, and would need an explanation of why they were not used.

Artistic evidence is not always clear, though three of the figures on the Franks casket – one of whom is probably the legendary dragon-slayer Sigurd – wear helmets which bear a striking resemblance to the reconstructed Coppergate example, complete with nasals. More basic iron helmets of a similar segmented 'spangenhelm' design

116

were common in Western Europe from late Roman times until the twelfth century, and it would be surprising if they had not made an appearance in England, but no examples have so far been found. They were constructed from a number of iron plates – usually four – riveted together by metal bands running across the crown, and could be made with or without a nasal to protect the face. By the eleventh century helmets seem to have become much more common, and the laws of King Cnut (reigned 1016–35) regard them as standard equipment for everyone serving in his armies, but paradoxically less physical evidence survives from this era. Not only were pagan-style burials with grave goods no longer in favour, but the very common-place nature of what were becoming mass-produced items militated against their survival. A plain 'spangenhelm' which was no longer required as armour might make a useful cooking pot until it finally disintegrated!

A few of the men on the Franks casket have very obvious sculpted hair, which suggests that those who do not are wearing some sort of soft headgear. It is possible that these, and the plain caps shown in other sources, could have been made of boiled leather or similar perishable material, which would have provided some protection to men unable to afford metal helmets while leaving no trace in the archaeological record.

Surviving body armour is even rarer than helmets, although again there is written and artistic evidence for its use. In Anglo-Saxon England it took the form of the mail coat or 'byrne' made of interlinked iron rings – a type of armour which seldom survives even from later periods when we know it was common. The only known example from our period comes from the Sutton Hoo burial, but, as in the case of helmets, there is no reason to suppose that it was restricted to men of the very highest rank. Two of the figures on the Franks casket lid, and one on the rear panel which depicts a column of Roman soldiers attacking Jerusalem, are wearing tunics which almost certainly represent mail, shown as a pattern of solid raised dots. This is a proportion of about one in five, depending on exactly who we interpret as being a combatant in these carvings. A similar pattern appears on one of two armed men depicted on the silver plate from the Staffordshire Hoard which is believed to have formed part of a helmet.

Battle Tactics

There is a common assumption that Anglo-Saxon battle tactics were of the very simplest kind. One writer refers to 'an alarming absence of tactical sense', considering that once battle was joined 'it was merely might, determination and often numbers which decided the day' (Heath). Contemporary sources certainly give this impression, although they are difficult to interpret because their authors were seldom interested in the details of military science. For Bede, for example, strategy and tactics were entirely redundant, as battles were decided by the will of God. Therefore battles usually went in favour of the most devout Christian commander, though occasionally the divine verdict might be reversed as a punishment for His worshippers' sins. (The career of Penda, as a consistently successful pagan general, must have been an embarrassment to Bede's world view, but he offers no explanation for it.)

In other cases battles are described according to the conventions of epic poetry, which have sometimes been mistaken by modern commentators for sober tactical analysis. A prominent example is the 'shieldwall', a term used almost universally nowadays as if it described a standard Anglo-Saxon formation, or even a tactical doctrine. As mentioned above, two quite different terms are routinely translated as 'shieldwall': 'bordweall' ('wall of boards') and 'scyldburh' ('fortress of shields'). The impression gained from these translations is that 'shieldwall' was a term in early English military parlance with a definite meaning. We might even imagine a commander giving his troops the order, 'Form shieldwall!' as modern re-enactment groups have been known to do. But no contemporary source describes any order given in these terms. Earl Byrhtnoth at Maldon told his men to 'make a war-hedge with their shields' ('he mid bordum het wyrcan thone wihagan'), but although both the 'shieldwall' terms occur elsewhere in the poem they are notably absent here where we might expect them.

118

There are also practical difficulties with the shieldwall as a formation. It is usually portrayed as consisting of a solid block of men standing in close order with shields overlapping, as Harold's huscarles seem to be doing on the Bayeux tapestry. Such a deployment has its advantages: it can present an unbroken line of spearpoints which will deter cavalry, as it was no doubt intended to do at Hastings, and the men can protect each other from missiles with their shields. But it is only useful on the defensive, as it is almost impossible to manoeuvre in such a close-packed mass – especially if the ground is at all uneven – unless the men are drilled in marching in step, for which there is no evidence from Anglo-Saxon times. Furthermore, although spears can be thrust straight forward fairly effectively, there is no room to wield swords without endangering one's comrades. The use of the shield boss as an offensive weapon would also involve breaking up the 'wall' and exposing the men on either side. We must therefore conclude that a battle between two English armies, both of which employed a 'shieldwall' formation, could never have been decisive, as both would have had to stand on the defensive. Attacks must have been carried out, and combats actually fought, in a looser, more open formation which allowed men to use their weapons as they were intended. Most writers concede that this was the case, but few give much thought to exactly how a close-packed shieldwall could be opened up while in action. It may have happened automatically as soon as the army advanced, as a result of the less eager or less well-equipped men hanging back slightly while their braver comrades pushed forward.

An example of this in Scandinavian warfare comes from 'Eyrbyggja Saga', where the opposing commander threw a spear over the heads of Snorri's warriors as they advanced uphill. This was a ritual act, intended to consign the enemy to the wrath of Odin, but in this case the spear hit and wounded a man who was lurking in the rear: Snorri's reaction was that this was a good thing, as it would show his men that hiding at the back was not always the safest option! And yet, assuming that the army would start the battle with the best-equipped men in the front rank, it would hardly have been consistent with either honour or military effectiveness to allow

119

them to abandon this position. The result of a free-for-all advance might have been that the elite, weighed down with their armour, would have been left behind by their more lightly armed followers – or worse still, jostled and pushed to the ground. So we must imagine the army moving forward in loose formation, but still in some kind of order, and the only way to do that would seem to be to extend the line to the flanks. Again this might happen without a specific order being given, as the men on the ends of the line would be reluctant to allow the enemy to outflank them, and so would be inclined to drift outwards as they advanced to prevent this. The process would be helped if the younger, fitter and perhaps more lightly equipped men were posted on the flanks, but we have no contemporary evidence for this.

Neither, apart from a few hints such as Henry of Huntingdon's account of the Battle of the River Idle, or Penda's thirty 'legions' at the Winwaed, can we tell from our sources whether the different contingents which made up an Anglo-Saxon army were capable of manoeuvring independently of each other. If battles were decided by any kind of tactical ploy the sources seldom if ever say so, though this may be due to several factors: surviving informants might not have seen enough of the field to know what was going on on the flanks, or clerical writers might have been indifferent to such technicalities, or war leaders themselves could have preferred to be remembered for their courage or personal fighting skills rather than what might have been seen as underhand tricks. The Battle of Chester in 605 appears to have been won by a Northumbrian charge at a weak spot – the Welsh monks who were praying for victory – followed by a swift wheel and an attack on the Welsh main body from an unexpected direction. But we cannot tell from Bede's account whether or not this was deliberate, and as usual the chronicler is more concerned to reveal the workings of God's plan to punish the Welsh heretics than to explain the minutiae of tactics.

In actual combat, as opposed to pre-battle manoeuvres, Anglo-Saxon warriors generally, if not invariably, operated on foot, though the question of whether they ever fought on horseback has been vigorously debated. Horses and horse riding are mentioned frequently in most of our sources, but remains of the animals are rare in agricultural contexts, and it is likely that they were kept mainly for military purposes. Several mentions in contemporary sources of what appear to be royal stud farms tend to confirm this (Davis, in Hawkes). Mound Seventeen at Sutton Hoo contained the skeleton of a horse which may have been sacrificed to accompany its late owner, as well as a magnificent and expensive set of harness. It is often stated that Anglo-Saxon warriors would have ridden ponies too small to be effective warhorses, but the Sutton Hoo horse was a respectable fourteen hands.

In the pre-Viking era, when armies were small and made up overwhelmingly of professional fighters, most campaigning armies would probably have been entirely mounted, which makes the success of lightning raids such as Wulfhere's attack on the Isle of Wight in 661 easier to understand. In fact the Anglo-Saxon Chronicle tells us that the Vikings of the eighth and ninth centuries made use of captured horses on their overland raids, implying that the English forces which pursued and often caught them must also have ridden rather than walked. Mounted warriors could sometimes ride down fugitives or raiders who were taken unawares, as happened to the Vikings outside Chester in 893. A plaque on the Sutton Hoo helmet shows a scene of a mounted spearman attacking enemy footsoldiers, and the Aberlemno Stone, a monument thought to commemmorate the Battle of Nechtansmere in 685, suggests that the Northumbrians deployed some mounted troops in their wars against the Picts. This suggestion may be supported by the mention of Northumbrian 'equitatui' or horsemen in the 'Life of Saint Wilfred', but this term could refer simply to men who rode on the march but dismounted to fight. Too much weight has perhaps been placed on the remark of Florence of Worcester that an English force fled from the Welsh in Herefordshire in 1055 because they had been ordered to fight from horseback, 'contra mores', or 'contrary to their custom'. This was an isolated and very late incident involving local levies fighting alongside French and Norman contingents, so it cannot be taken as good evidence for either English cavalry or English ineptitude.

Nevertheless, there is no convincing evidence for the use of large bodies of cavalry in pitched battles, at least before the eleventh century. We can be certain that if the English did not use cavalry it was not because they were unfamiliar with the idea. Contacts between the English kingdoms and the Franks on the Continent had been frequent since the sixth century, and the many English exiles living at the Carolingian court can hardly have failed to observe the increasing popularity of cavalry tactics in the Frankish armies. However, it has been suggested that even in the Frankish Empire in the tenth century the rise of cavalry was due more to the decline of the infantry than to any improvement in the effectiveness of mounted tactics (Nicolle). If this was the case it is possible that the English failed to adopt cavalry not because of ignorance or conservatism, but because they did not need to. They remained effective as infantry, and had already perfected the technique of manoeuvring mounted and fighting dismounted which was to be characteristic of English armies in the later medieval period.

The experience of a great battle must have been unforgettable, even for those, like the veterans of Penda's wars or the late ninth-century campaigns against the Danes, who had seen it all before. There would surely have been an important element of theatre in the preliminaries, with the waving banners and the gleaming gold and silver decoration of the thegns' equipment designed to overawe the enemy as much as to impress their comrades. It might have been possible to detect a big army even before it was in sight by the gleam of sunlight on its armour, as was said of the Vikings at Stamford Bridge in 1066. The opposing lines would probably have closed at a steady walking pace, imposed by the need to keep the lines straight, as well as by the difficulty of negotiating rough and perhaps slippery ground in smooth-soled leather footwear. The advance would almost certainly have been accompanied by chants or war cries, with the aim of frightening the enemy and encouraging your own forces to move together in time to the rhythm. Men might have competed to shout out the names of their gods or rulers, especially against an opponent of a different religion. It is hard not to be reminded of the rival slogans of the Norwegians at Stiklarstadir in 1030: 'On, on, farming men!' 'On, on, Christ's men, cross men, king's men!'

A passage in *Beowulf* implies that this phase of the battle would be remembered for the 'iron shower' of arrows sent on a high trajectory over the shields of the men in front to wound those behind. The 'shieldwall' might have seemed to waver as warriors raised and lowered their shields to intercept the missiles, giving observers an opportunity to assess their steadiness. Men with a reputation to make or maintain might nevertheless have braved the arrows and stepped out from the ranks to harangue their followers or insult the enemy, before charging forward to strike a blow in the sight of their king. At Maldon, if the poet is to be believed, the Mercian Aelfwine recounted his ancestry in true heroic style before rushing forward to stab a Viking with his spear. Then the lines would clash, men stabbing viciously downwards over their opponents' shields until their spears broke or an enemy got too close for them to be effective, then drawing their swords.

Graphic proof of the brutal nature of hand-to-hand fighting comes from skeletons excavated from various sites around the country. Six burials from a cemetery of apparently seventh-century date at Eccles in Kent were of men, mostly in their twenties or early thirties, who had suffered head injuries, probably from sword cuts: the lack of any evidence of healing shows that all of them had died either immediately or soon afterwards (Wenham, in Hawkes). One man had been struck in his unshielded right side by a spear or arrow, which had left its point in his spine and presumably disabled him before he received the coup de grace. Another had been virtually cut to pieces, with three wounds to his arms, ten to his back and no fewer than sixteen to the head and neck, several of which had almost severed his head. Probably he had been one of the last to fall, fighting on despite being surrounded and finally succumbing to a rain of blows from all directions. Perhaps he had made such an impression on his enemies by his determined stand that they needed to make sure that he would not get up again, and continued to hack at him when he lay on the ground. All the victims had been struck on the front or top of the head, mostly from the left side, which would be consistent with an attack by a right-handed swordsman. It is of course possible that they had suffered other wounds to the soft tissues, especially from arrows or spear thrusts, which would not be detectable from the skeletal remains.

A young man buried in Mound Five at Sutton Hoo also probably represents a battle casualty: he had been partially cremated, but a surviving piece of his skull shows that he had suffered at least nine serious cuts to the head (Carver). Another skeleton, excavated at Repton and identified by the sword and silver Thor's hammer amulet found with him as a ninth-century Viking, was presumably the victim of Anglo-Saxon wrath. He had been around 40 years old when he died, probably as a result of a deep cut to the left thigh. His skull also showed the marks of two blows to the head, and other damage suggested that he had been both disembowelled and castrated, though whether deliberately or as an incidental result of the attack which killed him is not known (Biddle and Kjolbye-Biddle). This gruesome evidence is supported by written accounts. Those from Anglo-Saxon sources are scarce, though at the Battle of Maldon a thegn named Eadweard is said to have brought down a Viking with a single sword cut. Norse sagas are full of stories of mighty blows which severed heads, arms or legs, and Beowulf had a sword which was said to have often sliced through helmets. This, of course, is the common currency of legend, reminiscent of later epics such as the 'Chanson de Roland', in which champions on both sides smash through armour with such regularity that one wonders why anyone bothered to wear it. On the other hand, modern experiments have shown that early medieval swords were easily capable of cutting right through animal carcasses similar in size to human bodies (Loades).

It is unlikely that the fittest warrior could fight hand to hand in armour for more than a few minutes without needing to rest, and the battle lines must have drawn apart at intervals to regroup and assess their chances. Where the sides were evenly matched the struggle might be brought to a close only by nightfall or mutual exhaustion, which might explain those cases like Offa's encounter at Otford in 776, where the Anglo-Saxon Chronicle mentions a battle but gives no indication of the outcome. The leaders might then have arranged a truce. Kings and leading noblemen often fought in the front rank, and their deaths could demoralise their followers and bring about their defeat. We hear of numerous cases in which a king was killed and his army slaughtered, but it is often difficult to sort out cause and effect, and decide whether the army collapsed because of the loss of its commander, or the king was left unprotected when those around him ran away.

The Aftermath of Battle

From Bede's stories we do know that the bodies of kings were usually recovered from the battlefield by their followers, and buried with ceremony. The mutilated warrior from Mound Five at Sutton Hoo was most likely a pagan, as both the date and the cremation rite suggest, so it was clearly not just the Christian war dead who were treated with reverence. Other casualties were no doubt carried off by relatives or surviving comrades in arms, and probably interred in groups close to the site of the battle, like the six bodies from Eccles. An army which had been driven from the field would of course have little opportunity to recover its dead or wounded, and the enemy rank and file seem to have been left where they lay. The Anglo-Saxon Chronicle's poem on the Battle of Brunanburgh preserves the gruesome details of their fate. It tells us that the characteristic scavengers of the battlefield were the raven, the white-tailed eagle and the wolf, the same trilogy that appears in *Beowulf*, where the raven 'tells the eagle of his takings at the feast.' These creatures of ill omen might follow an army for days in expectation of being fed. It was said in 'Y Gododdin' of the Welsh hero Caradwg that 'the motion of his arm invited the wild dogs', the idea being that the wolves knew his exploits so well that they would gather as soon as they saw him draw his sword.

Fortifications, Earthworks and Sieges

The fortified camps of the Vikings, and the 'burghs' which Alfred the Great and his successors built to counter them and subdue the territory which the invaders had overrun, were a vital feature of tenth-century warfare in England, but before that the role of fortifications seems to have been much more limited. We have seen how Aethelbald introduced the obligation to supply labour for fortress work, and there are cases such as the same king's siege of Somerton in 733 which imply the existence of fortified strongholds, but it was much more common for armies to seek decisive battles in the open than to attempt to fight from such positions. Where fortifications did feature in the Mercian Wars they seem to have been either simple palisaded banks and ditches, or the remains of forts surviving from the Roman era. Linear earthworks or dykes, apparently sited to control movement along the Roman roads, have been found in several locations around the western, southern and eastern borders of Mercia. Apart from Offa's Dyke on the frontier with Powys, which is discussed in more detail on pages 136 to 140, these include Wansdyke ('Woden's Dyke') on the border with Wessex, and Grim's Dyke ('Devil's Dyke') between Mercia and East Anglia. However, we hear of no military actions being fought on these defensive lines, and it is unlikely that they were ever more than symbolic barriers. The remains of similar earthworks have been detected around important sites such as Tamworth, and probably enclosed most if not all royal estates.

A feature of the Anglo-Saxon landscape which is often forgotten was the presence of Roman buildings in various states of dilapidation. Some Roman fortifications may still have performed their original function, though Asser's account of the battle at York in 867 makes it clear that the walls of the city had not been maintained, and so were not a significant obstacle to the attackers. Elsewhere the ruins of Roman towns and villas were useful mainly as a source of building materials. The Church of All Saints at Brixworth in Northamptonshire, for example, was probably built during or soon after the reign of Offa, and 'is now generally considered to be the largest and finest building of that period in Europe north of the Alps' (Pryor, 2006). The probable location of the church councils or synods at 'Clofesho' organised by Aethelbald and Offa from 747 onwards, this is the only surviving building in the country of which it can be said that the Mercian kings actually sat within the same walls that we do today.

It is constructed in large part of stone, bricks and tiles taken from the Roman ruins of Leicester and Towcester (Brooks). In fact its design seems to have been based on a Roman public building or basilica, and it does strike the modern viewer as somewhat 'Byzantine' in appearance. This was undoubtedly an exceptional edifice, which presumably owed its existence to the presence of a Mercian royal estate nearby, and most non-religious buildings seem still to have been of timber construction, like the great halls in *Beowulf*. But it does explain how churches in the Viking period, such as the one at Repton (see page 169), were sometimes strongly built enough to be used as temporary fortifications.

The role of such buildings was all the more important because the techniques of siege warfare were poorly developed. Gildas describes the first Saxon invaders as bringing down city walls with battering rams and throwing high towers to the ground, but neither archaeology nor other documentary sources suggest that they were capable of such feats. However, a miracle story recounted by Bede sheds some interesting light on the methods which might have been used to attack towns and other defended positions. At some time while Saint Aidan was bishop at Lindisfarne (so between 634 and his death in 651) Penda's Mercians had penned up the Northumbrians in their stronghold at Bamburgh, but had been unable to take the place either by storm or by conventional siege techniques. One problem was that Bamburgh was built on the sea shore, and so could not be blockaded by a purely land-based army. Penda therefore ordered all the nearby villages to be demolished and the wooden beams, rafters and wall panels, as well as the straw used for thatching the roofs, brought to Bamburgh. His troops piled all this inflammable material against the wall on the landward side, and as soon as the wind was favourable they set fire to it. This implies that at that time what Bede calls the 'city wall' may still have been a wooden palisade rather than a stone construction. The Anglo-Saxon Chronicle describes how Bamburgh was first fortified by King Ida, who reigned from 547 to 560, and was 'first enclosed by a stockade and thereafter by a wall', but gives no date for the replacement of the stockade. According to Bede, Aidan was praying in his hermitage on the Farne Islands, several miles offshore, when he saw the fire and smoke about to engulf the town, and cried out in alarm, 'Lord, see what evil Penda does!' The wind immediately changed direction and blew the flames back towards the Mercians, who were so demoralised that they abandoned the siege. Bede's motive of course was to establish Aidan as a bona fide English saint, and a modern rationalist might not consider that an unpredictable wind on the Northumbrian coast requires a supernatural explanation, but it is interesting that the defenders appear to have had no physical means of countering such an obvious method of attack.

Penda's tactic was in fact a large-scale version of a common theme in early English and Scandinavian warfare – attacks on, and burning of, wooden halls. The lid of the Franks casket seems to show such an attack, which is also described by the fragmentary poem known as 'The Fight at Finnsburh'. The date and author of this fragment are unfortunately unknown, but the poem appears to relate an event alluded to in *Beowulf*, which might date it to around the fifth century. King Hnaef and his war band are besieged in their mead hall, which they defend for five days against attempts to force a way through the doors, until one man is seriously wounded and leaves his post. Such a stalemate would usually end with the attackers trying to burn down the hall, an event also mentioned in *Beowulf*. According to Henry of Huntingdon, Caedwalla's brother Mul was killed in Kent in 687 in just such a hall-burning incident. He had gone out on a pillaging expedition accompanied by only twelve men; when surprised by the locals, he was forced to take refuge in the house which he was ransacking. He and his companions defended the doors until the enemy lost patience and set fire to the hall, burning Mul and all his men to death. On other occasions prolonged blockade seems to have been the only way to reduce a stoutly defended strong-point. Henry of Huntingdon describes elsewhere how Aethelbald, in his campaign against Somerton in 733, simply surrounded the place 'with camps all round', preventing supplies getting to the garrison. Eventually, realising that no relief force was coming, they surrendered.

Chapter 8

'The Glory of Britain'

It is indicative of the great changes that had taken place in the century since the death of Penda that although we know almost nothing about Penda apart from his military exploits, the reverse is true of Offa. By the time the latter came to the throne there were many other, less warlike, ways for a king to earn a reputation. The regularity with which Penda destroyed his rival kings reminds us of a hero of the ancient sagas, whereas his even more famous successor is depicted in the surviving sources as a diplomat, builder, administrator and patron of religion, but as a warlord hardly at all. William of Malmesbury notes that he could be successful in war when necessary, but was prepared to use subterfuge and even treachery if he thought it would bring more certain results. William, however, was prejudiced against Offa, and describes him as a 'pilferer' who had stolen wealth from churches, including the chronicler's own church at Malmesbury, to maintain his power. Asser described how Offa 'struck all the kings and regions around him with terror', and to Henry of Huntingdon he was 'a most warlike king, for he was victorious in successive battles over the men of Kent, and the men of Wessex, and the Northumbrians', but there is little solid evidence to support this rhetoric.

In more contemporary sources we are told that he seized power by the sword, and we know that his armies campaigned as far afield as Kent and North Wales, but we have no detailed account of any battle at which he is known to have commanded. This may in part reflect the times in which he lived. It seems from battle accounts that late eighth- and ninth-century Anglo-Saxon kings were less likely to be killed in combat than their seventh-century predecessors, and examples of them escaping from a defeat become more common. We should not necessarily imagine them remaining safely in the rear, but if kings of Offa's generation still led from the front, they were perhaps no longer expected to decide the battle by their personal heroics.

Once the unhappy Beornred had been put to flight, Offa inherited relatively intact the wide-ranging hegemony established by Aethelbald. Inevitably, however, his neighbours had taken advantage of the succession dispute and the accession of a new and untried young king. The Welsh Annals record a battle between 'Britons and Saxons' at Hereford in 760 which must represent an otherwise unknown Welsh invasion, and there is evidence that the West Saxons seized territory north of the Thames around Cookham in Berkshire at around the same time (Kirby). Beornred had fled to Northumbria and may have continued to carry out raids into Mercia, because Matthew of Westminster records that he burned the unidentified town of Cataracta in 769, and in the same year himself 'perished miserably' by fire. Possibly he was the accidental victim of one of his own incendiary attacks, or he may have been captured and disposed of in a way that his victims thought appropriate.

The Challenge from Kent

London and Essex appear to have remained loyal to Offa, whose charters show him giving away land at Harmondsworth, Twickenham and Woking with no reference to any local rulers. But the death of King Aethelberht in 762 may have precipitated a crisis in Kent, because two years later Offa arrived in person at Canterbury, where he issued a grant of land in his own name to the Bishop of Rochester. This is significant because until then the Mercian kings had been content to control Kent indirectly, through compliant members of the local dynasty. Around this time there were several candidates for the throne of Kent, one of whom, Heahberht, appears in Offa's entourage at Canterbury as a witness to the charter, and may have been the Mercian protégé.

130

The situation remained unclear, however, and it is likely that Offa, at the end of a long supply line and with commitments on other frontiers, was forced to compromise. Another charter in 765 was witnessed by two 'kings of Kent', Heahberht and Ecgberht, as well as by Offa. The latter had obviously reverted to the old policy of ruling through local nominees, but the Kentish kings quickly began to assert their independence, and later in the same year Ecgberht and Heahberht were issuing their own charters which made no mention of their Mercian overlord. Heahberht died in about 771 and Ecgberht took control of the whole kingdom, a move which may have been seen in Mercia as an unacceptable challenge to Offa's hegemony. Simeon of Durham says that in that year an army under Offa's command penetrated as far south as the Sussex coast, where he defeated the men of Hastings. This was a long way from the accepted Mercian sphere of influence, and the campaign may have been prompted by the fear that Kent was becoming the centre of a rival power bloc in the south-east.

In 776 Offa returned to Kent with an army, and the Anglo-Saxon Chronicle records that a great battle was fought between the Mercians and the inhabitants of Kent at Otford, three miles north of Sevenoaks. The name Otford derives from an earlier 'Ottanford', which might be a corruption of 'Offanford', preserving a memory of the place where the Mercian invader coming from the west would have crossed the River Darent. The Chronicle mentions 'a red sign of Christ in the heavens' and a plague of snakes in Sussex, which may have been interpreted as portents, but strangely omits to record the outcome of the battle itself. Henry of Huntingdon says that after the usual 'dreadful slaughter on both sides' Offa was victorious, but Stenton and most other modern scholars doubt this.

For the next decade the kings of Kent continued to grant charters as if they were entirely independent, making no reference to Offa at all. It is possible that the battle was a tactical stalemate, but that this was enough to secure a strategic victory for the men of Kent. Especially if their losses had been heavy, the Mercians might have been forced to withdraw northwards towards London in order to secure their lines of communication. The wonders reported by the

Chronicle may even be seen as signs of unusual weather in south-eastern England that year, which could have made it harder to feed the army. In that case Offa may have been happy to receive a purely nominal offer of submission from his opponents, which allowed him to claim a victory while leaving them de facto free of Mercian control.

Meanwhile Wessex had apparently also thrown off its subjection to Mercia during the early years of Offa's reign. Setting aside a collection of charters which seem to be later forgeries, there is no evidence that the West Saxon King Cynewulf, who had been a visitor to Aethelbald's court before his death in 757, gave the same allegiance to Offa (Stenton). But in 779 the Mercians moved to recover the lands north of the River Thames which had been lost early in the reign. Offa and Cynewulf met in battle near Benesington, which is usually identified with Benson in Oxfordshire, a few miles north of Wallingford. Benson was a West Saxon royal estate located on the stretch of the Thames which flows south-east from Oxford towards Reading, not far from the ford which gave Wallingford its name. It was presumably its strategic location rather than its intrinsic value which gave this settlement its importance. The two armies seem to have fought around the town, and at the end of the day it was in Mercian hands. The result of the battle was clearly more far-reaching, however, because most of Berkshire returned to Offa's control for the remainder of his reign. When Cynewulf died in 784 he was succeeded by Beorhtric, who became Offa's son-in-law and seems to have accepted a subordinate position as a Mercian ally. Northumbria, meanwhile, was also friendly if not formally subjugated. In 774 the Northumbrian king Ahlred was deposed and replaced by Aethelred, son of Moll, whom Stenton believed was virtually a Mercian puppet. Offa may even have been behind the coup, and have alluded to it in his self description in the same year, in another of his charters, as 'king of all England'.

After the Battle of Hereford Offa had regained the initiative against the Welsh, and the Welsh Annals describe the 'devastation' inflicted by Mercian campaigns against the 'South Britons' in 778 and against 'Britain' in general in the summer of 784. Having pre-empted any threat to his western frontier, Offa turned south-east once again to deal with Kent. Ecgberht had now died and had been succeeded as king by Ealhmund, but in 785 the latter abruptly disappeared from history and Offa began to grant lands in Kent on his own authority as he had at the beginning of his reign. No military campaign is recorded, but it seems likely that the Mercians had taken advantage of the change of ruler to launch a surprise attack, and that the sudden appearance of a Mercian army in Kent before he had a chance to consolidate his rule had obliged Ealhmund to submit.

This move was followed by a subtle rewriting of history, for in another famous charter Offa revoked a grant of land made by Ecgberht on the grounds that the latter had had no right to dispose of it, as he was not an independent ruler but only one of Offa's thegns (Whitelock). Kirby argues that the invasion may have been essentially defensive, intended to prevent the establishment of a Kentish hegemony in the south-east which could have threatened Offa's control of London and even taken the whole region into the orbit of Wessex. The evidence for this is twofold: firstly, charters suggest that Mercian control in Sussex followed a similar path to that in Kent, vanishing after Otford and being restored only in the late 780s. The Anglo-Saxon Chronicle also hints at some sort of emerging confederation which had been broken up by the Mercians: under the year 823 it records how the people of Kent and Surrey, as well as the East and South Saxons, welcomed the arrival of the West Saxon prince Aethelwulf 'because earlier they had been wrongly forced away from his relatives.' This Aethelwulf, according to an addition to the Chronicle for the year 784, was the grandson of Ealhmund of Kent.

Offa's difficulties with Kent prompted an interesting if ultimately unsuccessful experiment. England, then as now, was divided into two archbishoprics, the senior based at Canterbury and the other at York. Canterbury had been chosen in the early days of the con-version, despite the Pope's initial preference for London, because of its location in the kingdom of Kent, which was ruled by the first of the Anglo-Saxon royal dynasties to accept Christianity. In the eighth century the church was a powerful political force, and it must have rankled with Offa that while his Northumbrian counterparts had an archbishop under their control at York, he had not. Jaenberht, the Archbishop of Canterbury, appears to have been hostile to Offa and may even have been regarded as an instigator of anti-Mercian unrest. A campaign was therefore launched to persuade Pope Hadrian that the English bishops and clergy were eager to see a third archbishopric established in England. A papal delegation was sent to Offa, and – in what the Chronicle describes as a 'contentious' synod at Chelsea – Jaenberht found himself deprived of part of his archbishopric in favour of Offa's nominee Hygeberht, who was appointed Archbishop of Lichfield.

Aethelberht the Martyr

East Anglia, still ruled by the descendants of Raedwald, seems to have accepted Mercian overlordship peacefully since the time of Aethelbald, but towards the end of Offa's reign an incident occurred which has affected his reputation ever since. In 794 the young king of the East Angles, Aethelberht, travelled to Mercia to ask for permission to marry Offa's daughter. The bare bones of the story appear in the Anglo-Saxon Chronicle, which states that 'Here Offa ordered King Aethelberht's head to be struck off.' Several later medieval lives of Saint Aethelberht, as he was to become, provide further details. The most elaborate of these was written by Osbert of Clare, who as prior of Westminster Abbey in late twelfth century had custody of Aethelberht's head, preserved there as a holy relic. Osbert was also an East Anglian, and so had an additional reason to portray the saint in a favourable light.

According to his account the young king was born in 779, so was no more than 15 years old at the time of his death. When he was 14 he had succeeded his father on the throne and had been urged to marry, but being a very serious and religious youth he had found it difficult to choose a suitable queen. Eventually his advisers suggested Offa's daughter Alfthrytha, and despite the objections of his mother, who distrusted the Mercians, the king decided to visit Offa and ask for her hand. Ignoring various ominous signs and portents along the way, he continued his journey and eventually arrived at Sutton near Hereford, where Offa's court was staying. According to Osbert, Alfthrytha saw him approaching at the head of his retinue and was impressed by his splendid appearance, but the girl's mother, Queen Cynefrith, apparently alarmed by her daughter's enthusiasm for the match, persuaded Offa that his guest was planning an invasion of Mercia. The king therefore ordered him to be seized and executed, entrusting the deed to a certain Winbertus, a wanted murderer who had taken refuge at court. Winbertus then asked Aethelberht to disarm before entering Offa's presence, shut him inside the hall and beheaded the boy with his own sword. The body was thrown into the River Lugg, but was later recovered after the usual miracles revealed its location. Offa was stricken with remorse and endowed various churches and monasteries by way of penance.

The story has become well known, but can hardly be accepted at face value. Even if we concede that Osbert or the source on which he drew preserved a genuine memory of events, their obvious East Anglian bias must be taken into account. The role of Cynefrith cannot be confirmed, and may be a device to avoid putting the blame for the crime onto a respected monarch such as Offa. Her husband had married two other daughters to the kings of Northumbria and Wessex, and can hardly have objected to another dynastic match as such, especially as Aethelberht is unlikely to have ridden across Mercia without some kind of invitation, or at least acknowledgement that his suit would be welcome. Offa may of course have deliberately lured him into a trap, but his motive is unclear. It has been pointed out that Aethelberht had begun to strike coins which, unlike previous East Anglian issues, omitted Offa's name, and that this might have been, or been mistaken for, a bid for independence. Osbert remarks in passing that an earthquake as the young king set out terrified 'the whole war band', which reminds us that no Anglo-Saxon king would have travelled without a substantial bodyguard. Perhaps his following was large and well equipped enough to be mistaken for an invading army, or at least to outnumber the troops at the Mercian court and give rise to genuine alarm. Whatever the

135

circumstances, Offa seems to have profited by the incident despite his alleged remorse, as Matthew of Westminster says that he immediately dispatched an army which brought the leaderless East Angles under his direct control.

Offa's Dyke

The achievement for which Offa is best known today is of course the building of the dyke bearing his name along the Welsh border. A great deal of attention has been given to the questions of how, why and exactly when Offa built this great earthwork – but much less to whether he actually built it at all. The evidence is surprisingly thin. The first documentary evidence comes from Asser's *Life of King Alfred*. Asser was writing in the 890s, more than a century after the generally accepted date for the construction of the dyke, and he mentions it only in passing. 'In fairly recent times', we are told, a 'vigorous king' of Mercia called Offa 'had a great dyke built between Wales and Mercia from sea to sea.' Several other medieval writers mention the dyke and associate it with Offa, including Simeon of Durham, Gerald of Wales and Walter Map. The first account written in Welsh appears to be the 'Brut y Saeson', which dates from the fifteenth century and describes the dyke as Offa's response to a series of Welsh raids in 783 and 784. However, these accounts are all much later than Asser and cannot be regarded as independent sources. Certainly various parts of the feature have long been known locally by names associating it with Offa, but this cannot be considered as proof unless we are also prepared to accept Wansdyke on the Wiltshire Downs, or Grim's Dyke east of Cambridge, as evidence for the personal involvement of Woden and the Devil.

It will be objected that Offa was a known historical figure, but his very eminence would tend to attract associations with anything mysterious in or on the frontiers of his kingdom. This process is evident even today: in 2009 and 2011, for example, the local press in Tamworth found Offa a useful asset in raising the profile of their campaign to keep the Staffordshire Hoard in the town. The hoard almost certainly predates his reign by at least 100 years, but Offa, as the only Mercian king most readers will have heard of, was an obvious headline-grabber. What is more, in the eighth and ninth centuries the phrase 'Offa's Dyke' would have had connotations entirely lost to later generations. The genealogies in the Anglo-Saxon Chronicle trace the descent of both Offa and Penda from Offa, son of Waermund, who was believed to have ruled in the Angles' Continental homeland twelve generations before his Mercian namesake. This 'Offa of Angeln' was a famous hero of Germanic legend, mentioned in *Beowulf* and in 'Widsith', which from its archaic language is thought to be the earliest surviving English poem (Stenton). According to the latter source, Offa, while still a young man, 'won by warfare the greatest of kingdoms', generally identified with the base of the Jutland Peninsula and the region of the River Eider in North Germany. Here, the poem continues, 'he set out the boundary against the Myrgings, by Fifeldor, and ever thereafter they held it, the Angles and the Swabians, as Offa struck it.' In other words his most lasting achievement was to establish a fixed boundary against a previously hostile neighbour; this most likely involved the building of some sort of fortified line 'from sea to sea', which was certainly how later generations interpreted the story.

If we are prepared to accept the idea that Offa of Mercia did not necessarily plan and build the immense work which bears his name from scratch, this removes many of the difficulties with its dating. It has always been difficult to identify any point in his reign, or in those of his predecessors and successors, when the military situation would have justified such an undertaking. As we have seen, a late Welsh source states that it was built in response to Welsh raids in the 780s, but the more closely contemporary Welsh Annals records only English invasions of Wales during this period. If the dyke was really built at this time, the Mercian armies were pushing beyond it almost as soon as it was completed. Furthermore, recent archaeological work has led to little agreement on the nature and function of the dyke, which is understandable if different sections were built by different groups for their own various purposes. Less than a fifth of the course of the dyke runs along current parish boundaries, which has been used as evidence that it was in fact driven through by a single ruthless leader, dividing communities where military strategy dictated, regardless of local sensitivities (Fox). However, this argument only holds if the parishes were already in existence in the eighth century, which has not been proven. If they were not established until later, it may only indicate that the dyke was not considered a major obstacle.

Similarly, it has been pointed out that according to place name evidence, several long-established English-speaking settlements with names such as Thornbury, Woodiston and Downton were marooned on the western side. This is especially noticeable where the dyke runs east of the River Severn south of Welshpool, and south of the River Lugg between Knighton and Kington. This could be an indication of Offa's ruthlessness, abandoning fellow Englishmen to the enemy as part of a political compromise, or simply in order to keep the frontier on the most easily defensible line. Clearly the Welsh did not immediately descend from the hills and wipe them out, or their villages would not still retain their English names. On the other hand, it is hard to see why Offa would have needed to sacrifice any Mercian territory in view of his military predominance during this period.

One recent interpretation suggests that the central portion of the dyke, marking the border with the kingdom of Powys, was indeed a single construction undertaken by Offa in the 770s and 780s, but that other unrelated works gradually became associated with it, leading to Asser's mistaken belief that it extended 'from sea to sea' (Hill and Worthington). This theory accounts for many of the gaps and anomalies in the construction, but may still be stretching the evidence a bit too far. It relies first of all on the idea that a resurgent kingdom of Powys could have presented a threat to Mercia. The evidence for this comes from an inscription which was once legible on the Pillar of Eliseg, a monument to the king of that name which still stands a few miles north of Llangollen. As recorded in 1696 by Edward Lluyd, this stated that it had been erected by Eliseg's great-grandson Cyngen ap Cadell in honour of his ancestor, who had 'annexed the heritage of Powys throughout nine [years] from the power of the Saxons.' The end of Cyngen's reign can be dated to around 855, so it is quite likely that Eliseg was a contemporary of Offa, but there is no other evidence for his career, and his conquest (or reconquest) of Powys must have been only temporary. It is hard to believe that the 'vigorous' king Asser describes would have responded to the loss of a client kingdom by walling it off with a great defensive line, then immediately rendered it obsolete by sending his armies westwards again.

There is also the objection that even this section of the dyke cannot have been much use as a military obstacle. No trace has been found of a wooden palisade along the top of the bank, nor – despite a few unsubstantiated claims – of forts or watchtowers associated with the work. It is not even certain that the ditch was always on the western side, even in the central sector. Where there are the remains of a ditch on the eastern face, these are usually interpreted as incidental products of the construction process, perhaps where earth or turf was excavated to raise the height of the bank. However, there are stretches where the eastern ditch seems to have been deeper and better demarcated than the western one, which is hard to explain if it was built to keep out invaders coming from the west (Bapty). It has often been noted that for most of its course the dyke is carefully sited to overlook the terrain to the west, but this would be of very limited value unless it was continuously manned throughout its length.

With the current state of knowledge the easiest way to resolve most of these difficulties is to accept that most of the dyke as we know it is not a single coherent defensive line, but was created by linking up already existing earthworks of different origins. That these broadly followed the line of the Mercian–Welsh border is not surprising, as this corresponded to a geographical frontier between the English lowlands and the Welsh hills which had probably dictated political boundaries since pre-Roman times. It is also possible that some features never were linked to the main dyke, but have been associated with it by modern investigators who have taken Asser's 'sea to sea' remark too literally. At some point before Asser wrote, a powerful Anglo-Saxon ruler must have undertaken the formidable task of joining the works on the frontier with Powys into a single continuous line, but probably not with a narrowly military function in mind. The dyke looks more like a prestige project intended to overawe the peoples beyond, sited, perhaps, to be seen from afar rather than to provide a (non-existent) garrison with lines of sight to the west.

There is also reason to believe that the instigator of this project was not Offa himself but one of his predecessors. As we have seen, Offa went to great lengths to safeguard his rights to demand fortification work from his subjects, but although this explains how he could have mobilised the necessary manpower, similar obligations had existed before his reign. As discussed in Chapter 3, Aethelbald introduced compulsory fortification work and was even criticised by the church for trying to impose it on monastic houses. There is also evidence that the threat of attack from Wales was far greater at certain periods in the seventh and early eighth centuries. The Welsh poem celebrating Cynddylan's attack on Wall or Lichfield has already been mentioned (see page 65). According to Felix's *Life of Saint Guthlac*, between 704 and 709 the 'Britons, the dangerous enemies of the Saxon race, were oppressing the nation of the English with war, pillage and devastation of the people.' The Welsh Annals which recorded Offa's invasions also tell how in 722 'the Welsh won three battles,' and in 743 and 753 Aethelbald of Mercia and Cuthred of Wessex fought together against the Welsh. Unfortunately we are not told the location of any of these encounters, but the one fought at Hereford in 760, at the beginning of Offa's reign, shows that they need not necessarily have been on the western side of the frontier. In conclusion, then, it would not be surprising if Offa turned out to be only the last and best known of a succession of Mercian kings who built or strengthened earthworks along the Welsh frontier.

Offa's Towns
One of Offa's main strategic objectives in his campaigns in Kent and Sussex was undoubtedly to safeguard his occupation of London, which by the end of the eighth century was once again the principal port and market of southern England, as it had been in Roman

times. But the political heartland of Mercia remained where it had been in Penda's day, between the Birmingham Plateau and the Middle Trent Valley. The town of Tamworth, at the confluence of the Rivers Tame and Anker, lies about seven miles south-east of Lichfield and the same distance due east of Wall, and seems originally to have been known as Tomtun, a centre for the people referred to in the charters as the Tomsaetan or 'settlers by the Tame'. It may have been a Mercian royal estate as early as the 690s, as a document of that date from Peterborough records King Aethelred confirming a deed 'in his chamber in his own vicus called Tomtun' (Gelling). At this date it may have been just one of several places where the Mercian kings held their courts, but by the reign of Offa it was becoming the principal base for the festivities at Christmas and Easter, and from the 780s onwards Offa regularly issued his charters from there. In 781 the name of the town appears as 'Tamouorthige', incorporating the element 'worth' which is often thought to denote an enclosed or fortified settlement (Gelling). This suggests that the ditch and bank which has been partially excavated around the centre of the modern town was constructed by Offa in recognition of its growing importance. There is little or no evidence of trade or of a substantial civilian population, but it has been deduced that there must have been a church on the site, as an ostentatiously Christian king like Offa would hardly have spent the two most important festivals of the Christian year in a place where there was no opportunity to attend mass.

Another sign of the importance of the site is the discovery of a pair of eighth- to ninth-century water mills on the River Anker, which, as archaeologists have discovered from traces of grain, were used to grind oats and barley. Barley was the most common grain for bread making in the Anglo-Saxon period, but oats, although undoubtedly eaten by the poor, are unlikely to have been intended for human consumption at a royal palace. They may therefore indicate the presence of a large number of horses for use by the army, which had to be stabled within the enclosure and fed over the winter. Mill-stones have been excavated which seem to be made of volcanic stone from the Rhineland, possibly the 'black stones' which Offa is recorded as requesting from the Frankish emperor Charlemagne. Unfortunately no trace of Offa's 'palace' has yet been found, and it may lie underneath the present site of Saint Editha's Church in the centre of Tamworth. It is likely in any case to have been built of wood, and many writers have envisaged something like Hrothgar's great mead hall in *Beowulf*, a poem which may have been first performed at Offa's court: 'a house greater than men on earth had ever heard of'. Its fate, too, may ultimately have been the same once the days of Mercian glory were past: 'Boldly the hall reared its arched gables; unkindled the torch-flame that turned it to ashes.'

Much debate has centred around whether or not there were 'towns' in eighth-century Mercia, in the sense of organised communities with citizens engaged in occupations other than agriculture or government. There were, however, certainly substantial walled settlements which functioned as collection points for tribute and taxation, supply bases and probably as muster points for the army. Apart from Tamworth, Offa had such bases at Hereford, Stafford, Northampton and possibly elsewhere. Hereford was defended by a ditch similar in construction to that at Tamworth, while at Northampton traces have been found of a solidly built stone hall, one of the very few secular stone buildings in the country, the interior of which may once have looked similar to the Church of All Saints at Brixworth (see page 126). The settlement at Wall near Lichfield, where Penda may have had a similar base, is not heard of after the seventh century and may have been abandoned in favour of Saint Chad's foundation a few miles away, although a large number of archaeological finds from the site have yet to be published. Two other former Roman cities, Chester and Lincoln, still stood at the north-western and north-eastern corners of Mercia respectively, although in the early tenth century the walls of Chester seem to have been too dilapidated to be effective for defence. Lincoln had once been the capital of the independent district of Lindsey, a bone of contention between Mercia and Northumbria, but by Offa's reign it was firmly attached to the former, and Henry of Huntingdon quotes an anonymous verse which celebrates Lincoln as 'a noble city ... facing the south'.

Offa and Charlemagne

It was probably his involvement in Kent which brought about Offa's close relationship with the greatest figure in early medieval European history, the Frankish emperor Charlemagne. (He was not actually crowned emperor until the year 800, after Offa's death, but the title seems appropriate in view of his pre-eminence among the kings of Western Europe.) Charlemagne, or Charles the Great, became king of the Franks in 768, and over the following decades expanded his territory from its heartland in France and western Germany by means of campaigns in Brittany, Saxony, Spain, Italy, Bavaria, Bohemia and as far east as the Balkans. By the end of the eighth century he had established the first European superpower since the fall of Rome, and become one of the few secular figures outside Britain of whom the Anglo-Saxon Chronicle takes notice. The Northumbrians had sent envoys to the Frankish court as early as 773, and the Franks already had especially close relations with Kent, to whose ruling dynasty they were related by marriage (J. Nelson, in Brown and Farr). Mercia seems to have been relatively slow to cultivate contacts overseas, as might be expected from its inland location, but Matthew of Westminster says that in the 770s Offa was endeavouring 'to make a friend of Charlemagne' as a counter-balance to the hostility which his expansionist policies had aroused among his English neighbours.

Among Charlemagne's leading counsellors in the next two decades was the renowned Northumbrian scholar Alcuin of York, who arrived at his court in 782. Soon after that we have records of an ongoing correspondence between Alcuin and Charlemagne, on the one hand, and Offa on the other. It does not appear to have begun auspiciously. In a letter dated sometime after 784, Pope Hadrian wrote to Charlemagne acknowledging a missive in which the latter had tipped him off about a rumour relating to Offa. Apparently the Mercian king had found it necessary to warn his Frankish counterpart about a story, which alleged that Offa had tried to persuade Charlemagne to depose the Pope and replace him with a Frankish bishop. The context for this bizarre plot was probably the ill feeling between Offa and Archbishop Jaenberht and the king's attempts to obtain papal approval for his archbishopric at Lichfield. Hadrian clearly thought the rumour 'incredible' and accepted that unidentified enemies of Offa had spread it to discredit him, but it was not a promising start for Mercia's debut in the world of European diplomacy. More encouraging was a letter of introduction from Alcuin for a teacher who had been sent to Mercia at the king's request. After praising Offa for his interest in education, Alcuin goes on to flatter him in the most extravagant terms, which must presumably have been endorsed by his employer Charlemagne: 'You are the glory of Britain, the trumpet of proclamation, the sword against foes, the shield against enemies.'

Elsewhere Charlemagne addresses Offa as 'dearest brother' and 'friend', language which was fairly standard for correspondence between rulers at the time, but which has led some scholars (though only English ones, as Professor Nelson points out, in Brown and Farr) to argue that the Frankish king regarded Offa as his equal. In fact this is unlikely. In terms of size, military power and political prestige the Frankish Empire was of a different order of magnitude from Mercia even at its greatest extent. Charlemagne was well aware of this, and in his letters he always names himself first, and with numerous titles ('King of the Franks and Lombards, Patrician of the Romans'), in contrast to his correspondent, who is merely 'King of the Mercians'. There is a sense that Charlemagne is subtly trying to put Offa in his place, and what that place was is made clear by a diplomatic incident which occurred around 789.

The Frankish king had written to Offa requesting one of his daughters as a bride for his son Charles, and had sent Abbot Gervold of Saint Wandrille, a friend of both men, to negotiate the match. The almost contemporary *Deeds of the Abbots of Saint Wandrille* relates how Offa replied that he would agree on condition that Charlemagne's daughter Bertha was given to his own son in exchange. It seems from this that Offa was himself fooled by the language of diplomatic flattery and supposed that Charlemagne regarded him as a ruler of equal rank, but he soon realised his mistake. The Frankish king was angry at his presumption and ordered trade sanctions against England. This source claims that Gervold talked him out of it, but

144

one of Alcuin's letters refers to the temporary halting of trade across the English Channel, suggesting that the embargo was implemented, at least for a short time.

The rest of Offa's correspondence with Charlemagne deals mainly with routine matters such as the treatment of refugees from each other's kingdoms, religion, trade and the suppression of a racket which involved merchants posing as pilgrims in order to avoid paying tolls. Some issues mentioned in passing shed useful light on Offa's kingdom. Charlemagne sent him a gift of a belt and a 'Hunnish' sword, which may have been a weapon captured from the Avars, invaders from Central Asia like the earlier Huns, whom the Franks conquered in a series of campaigns between 789 and 796. This would have been a single-edged curved sabre of a type recently introduced into Europe by the Avars, and it would be interesting to know Offa's opinion of this novel design.

A complaint about the small size of English woollen cloaks is the first evidence for the export of wool, which was to become a main-stay of the later medieval economy and may have been so as early as the eighth century. Cloaks were a basic part of Frankish military costume, and it is surprising to find their ruler relying on Mercia to supply them. The emperor seems to have had something of an obsession about cloaks. Notker, in his *Gesta Caroli*, quotes his criticism of similar inadequate garments obtained from the Frisians (though they may have been the same ones, manufactured in England and imported by Frisian traders): 'What is the use of these little bits of cloth? ... When I am riding I cannot protect myself against the wind and rain. When I have to go and answer a call of nature, I suffer because my legs are frozen!' Other goods were also traded in grow-ing quantities during this period, and it is likely that the famous silver penny, the basis of English currency from Offa's time until the thirteenth century, was introduced, or standardised, in order to be acceptable in trade with the Frankish Empire.

The Coming of the Vikings

Probably the best-known entry in the whole of the Anglo-Saxon Chronicle relates how in the year 793, three years before Offa's

145

death, 'terrible portents' afflicted the land of Northumbria. First came great storms with flashes of lightning and 'fiery dragons', then a great famine, and finally, in June, the most ominous event of all: 'the raiding of heathen men miserably devastated God's church in Lindisfarne island by looting and slaughter.' (The Chronicle actually ascribes this raid to January, but this is an unlikely time of year for long sea voyages and the alternative date of June, based on the 'Annals of Lindisfarne', is more generally accepted (Swanton (trans.), *Anglo-Saxon Chronicle*, 1996).) Almost equally well known is the reaction of Alcuin of York, writing from the court of Charlemagne, to this news. 'Never before in Britain', he complained, 'has such a terror appeared as this we have now suffered at the hands of the heathen. Nor was it thought possible that such an inroad from the sea could be made.' This is usually regarded as the first appearance of the Vikings in England, a scourge which was to dominate the country's history for the next three centuries. But if Alcuin, and the brutal and ineffectual King Aethelred of Northumbria, were taken by surprise by the raid, there is evidence that Offa was not.

What the Chronicle calls 'the first ships of the Danish men' to appear in England had actually done so early in the reign of King Beorhtric of Wessex, who ruled from 786 to 802. The newcomers were in fact not Danes but Norwegians, from Hordaland in the region of Hardanger Fjord. They landed, according to the 'Annals of St Neots', on the island of Portland off the Dorset coast. Their presence was reported to the king's reeve in the nearby town of Dorchester, a man named Beaduheard, who assumed that they were traders and rode to meet them accompanied only by a handful of men. Beaduheard tried to order the Vikings to accompany him back to Dorchester, and was promptly killed.

Beorhtric was Offa's son-in-law and at least nominally his vassal, and there can be no doubt that this incident was reported to the Mercian king, who quickly realised what it implied. It must have taken place before 796, because some time between 792 and the end of his reign Offa issued a grant at one of the synods held at Clofesho exempting the church in Kent from certain obligations. Not included in the exemption – and therefore presumably considered as the

146

highest priority – were military service 'against pagan seamen with migrant fleets' and 'the construction of bridges and fortifications against the pagans'. So within a very short time of the first Viking raids, and possibly even before the attack on Lindisfarne, Offa had not only grasped the nature of the new threat, but had begun to put in place, in one of the most vulnerable parts of his realm, effective measures to deal with it. Whether the purpose of the bridges was purely for communication and rapid deployment, or whether they were also intended to block the raiders' passage up the rivers, we cannot be sure, but the use of fortifications foreshadows the development of defensive 'burghs' under Alfred the Great, and a well-planned system of walls and forts might have been effective if it had been completed in time. Offa in his prime could surely have carried out such a plan, but it was not to be.

The great king died on 29 July 796. A battle at Rhuddlan mentioned by the Welsh Annals in the same or the following year is sometimes thought to be connected with his death, but Offa must by now have been at least 60 years old, and it is unlikely that he was still leading his armies from the front. The chronicle attributed to Matthew of Westminster gives a more plausible account. It tells how Offa had built 'a most truly noble monastery' at St Albans to commemorate the discovery of what were supposed to be the remains of the early Christian martyr Alban. Soon afterwards he passed away at a nearby settlement 'which is called Offaeleia'. Apparently an attempt was made to bring his body back to the Mercian heartland, perhaps for burial at Repton, but according to the tradition preserved at St Albans it never arrived. The king was buried 'with royal magnificence' outside Bedford, where a chapel and a royal sepulchre were erected in his memory on the banks of the River Great Ouse. The course of this river shifts constantly, however, and by the time Matthew wrote in the fourteenth century the buildings had been swept away. It was said that it was still then possible when the water was low in summer to see the remains of the sepulchre lying on the bottom of the river, but the site has long since been lost. There are other candidates for the burial place, including Repton, Lichfield and Offlow in Staffordshire, and

147

Offchurch near Leamington Spa, but no archaeological evidence for any of them.

Offa had reigned for thirty-nine years, in itself a considerable achievement in that era. What is more, he had made careful arrangements for an orderly succession. Nine years earlier, at the great council held on the banks of the Thames at Chelsea, he had had his son Ecgfrith 'consecrated' as king by his puppet archbishop, Hygeberht. This represents an important step forward in the history of the English monarchy, as it is the first time that such a ceremony of consecration is known to have taken place. It was undoubtedly inspired by Frankish practice, and intended both to enhance the status of the kingship and to pre-empt any rival claims to the throne after Offa's death.

Nevertheless, this ambitious attempt to secure the future of the dynasty was destined to fail. Ecgfrith survived his father by only 141 days. The cause of his death on 17 December is not known, but there is no suggestion that he was overthrown by force. Alcuin attributed it to divine displeasure with the ruthless manner in which Offa had disposed of rivals to ensure his son's succession. 'This was not a strengthening of his kingdom,' he insisted, 'but its ruin.' Alcuin, of course, was not to know that Mercia was very far from ruined, but was to maintain its position among the leading powers of the British Isles for another three-quarters of a century. In some respects, its finest hour was yet to come.

Chapter 9

Offa's Successors and the Danish Invasions

Ecgfrith was an energetic young man, 'most noble' in Alcuin's estimation, and must have seemed a worthy successor to the great Offa. During his brief reign he issued charters granting land in at least three areas, including Wiltshire in the heart of Wessex. But almost immediately after his death, if not before, Mercia's subject kingdoms began to break away. Once again the details of the royal succession are unclear, but two years later a certain Coenwulf, claimed to be a descendant of Penda's brother Coenwalh and perhaps the best claimant left unscathed by Offa's purges, was firmly on the throne. From references in his own charters Coenwulf seems to have had family connections with the abbey at Winchcombe, near Cheltenham in Gloucestershire, where his daughter was the abbess and the king himself was later buried. This was the heartland of the old Hwiccan kingdom, and it has been suggested that Coenwulf was descended from the Hwiccan royal family as well as the Mercian, or even that his alleged Mercian ancestry was invented to bolster his claim to the throne (Zaluckyi). The Hwicce never seem to be referred to as a separate political entity after Coenwulf's accession, which strengthens the argument that with him the two royal lines were finally merged.

Whatever his origin, the new king established his authority with a ruthless energy worthy of his predecessors. In 798 the Anglo-Saxon Chronicle records him campaigning in Kent, which had declared its

149

independence under a former priest named Eadberht Praen, who had been living at Charlemagne's court as a refugee from the wrath of Offa. Coenwulf's first move was to persuade Pope Leo III to excommunicate Praen, so that he could not be accused of launching an attack on the church in the person of one of its ordained priests. Leading what Simeon of Durham calls 'the whole force of his army', Coenwulf then devastated Kent, especially the Romney Marsh area, captured Praen, and took him back to Mercia as a bound prisoner. Perhaps because he had once been a member of the clergy, the hapless rebel was not killed, but the Chronicle says that Coenwulf had him blinded and his hands cut off. William of Malmesbury records a story that the king later released Praen as an act of 'clemency' to mark the dedication of a church at Winchcombe, though the mutilated former rebel can hardly have been much of a threat, if indeed he ever had been.

The campaign of 798 incidentally brought about the end of Offa's short-lived archbishopric of Lichfield. When Praen began his rebellion Jaenberht's successor as Archbishop of Canterbury, a Mercian appointee named Aethelheard, fled to Rome, provoking a sarcastic remark from Alcuin about the 'good shepherd' who was supposed to lay down his life for his flock. Coenwulf took the opportunity to write to the Pope suggesting that the English church be reorganised into two archbishoprics at London and York, as Pope Gregory had originally planned at the time of Augustine's mission in 597. His motives no doubt had more to do with politics than religion, as the location of the head of the church at Canterbury had always been an obstacle to the suppression of Kentish independence, and London was far more securely under Mercian control. In exchange for this the king was prepared to abandon the archbishopric at Lichfield, which he now admitted had been a pet project of Offa's and lacked support from the English bishops. Archbishop Hygeberht, seeing how the wind was blowing, seems to have resigned his see before he could be sacked, but in the event Pope Leo refused to agree to the transfer to London, and in 802 confirmed Aethelheard in his post at Canterbury, effectively abolishing the post at Lichfield. Coenwulf was by then firmly back in control of

Kent, and perhaps for this reason did not pursue the matter. A key part of Offa's plan to maintain Mercian supremacy had thus been abandoned.

After the subjugation ('almost utter destruction', says Simeon of Durham) of Kent the victorious Mercian king appointed his brother Cuthred as his viceroy in the former kingdom. In 807, however, Cuthred died, and Coenwulf reimposed direct rule. Clearly a swift and decisive resolution of affairs in the south-east had been necessary, because trouble had also arisen on the western frontier. Apparently in the same year as the Kentish campaign, the Welsh Annals record that King Caradog of Gwynedd was killed 'by the Saxons'. As this source is prone to describe all English as 'Saxons', this is usually interpreted as another reprisal by Coenwulf against a bid for independence. We have no written sources for events in East Anglia, but for a brief period around 798 coins were struck there bearing the name of an otherwise unknown king named Eadwald. This may represent yet another doomed rebellion, rapidly suppressed in another whirlwind campaign in the hectic year or two following Coenwulf's accession (G. Williams, in Brown and Farr). In these three campaigns, in what may have been a single season, the Mercian army can hardly have travelled less than 500 miles.

Further trouble was to follow from another old enemy, Northumbria. The Anglo-Saxon Chronicle does not mention this war, but according to Simeon of Durham the unpopular Northumbrian king Aethelred had been assassinated in 796, to be succeeded by Osbald, who reigned for twenty-seven troubled days before abandoning his throne to a nobleman named Eardwulf. The latter was later to be canonised as Saint Eardwulf, but his holiness was not immediately apparent. While engaged in a purge of his rivals he discovered an alleged Mercian plot to depose him, and in 801 led an army against Coenwulf. The Mercian king mustered a large army which Simeon says included 'many forces from other provinces', though it is not clear whether this refers to traditional Mercian subjects such as the Hwicce or client kingdoms like Wessex and East Anglia. It is possible that Coenwulf was unsure of the loyalty of some of these contingents, because this campaign saw none of the ruthless action with which he was normally associated. Simeon describes a 'long campaign', terminated not by a decisive battle but by a negotiated peace, made at the urging of nobles and bishops from both sides.

On his southern front Coenwulf signed a treaty with Beorhtric of the West Saxons in 799, but three years later hostilities broke out when Beorhtric died and was succeeded by his old rival Ecgberht. The latter had been sent into exile during his predecessor's reign and was obviously regarded as anti-Mercian. William of Malmesbury relates how he had originally been given asylum at the Mercian court, but had been expelled as part of an agreement by which Beorhtric married Offa's daughter. It has also been suggested that Ecgberht was somehow involved in Eadberht Praen's rebellion (Zaluckyi). Mercian reaction was characteristically swift. The Anglo-Saxon Chronicle says that 'on the same day' as Ecgberht's accession an army of the Hwicce, led by Ealdorman Aethelmund but no doubt with Coenwulf's approval, crossed the River Thames into Wessex at Kempsford, a few miles north of the modern town of Swindon. From the Chronicle's brief account it seems that the Hwiccans were on horseback, and they may have been either a large raiding party or an advanced guard for the main Mercian army. We are told that they crossed the border, so it must have been somewhere south of the Thames that they encountered the 'Wiltshire men' under Ealdorman Weohstan. Although both sides were only local contingents and neither king was present, the ensuing clash is described as a 'big battle', and it was clearly bitterly contested. The commanders on both sides were killed, but the Wiltshire army was victorious. Perhaps as the defenders, fighting on home ground, they were able to muster more fighting men than the hastily organised raiders. This battle is the last recorded independent action of a Hwiccan army.

Despite this defeat, the next fourteen years of Coenwulf's reign seem to have been quiet. He had re-established the supremacy of Mercia south of the Humber, and although Ecgberht remained on the throne of Wessex his energies seem to have been directed mainly against the Britons of Cornwall. Then in 816 the Welsh Annals record the beginning of a series of wars in the west. In that year

152

'Saxons' attacked Rhufoniog and the 'mountains of Eyri' (Snowdonia) in North Wales. From the location the culprits must surely have been the Mercians, and the same source for the year 818 is more explicit, stating that Coenwulf devastated Dyfed in the south-west. Three years later Coenwulf died; the Anglo-Saxon Chronicle gives no details, but the Frankish writer Gaimar locates his death at Basingwerk in Flintshire. This implies that he was engaged in another Welsh campaign, but no battle is mentioned so it is likely that he died of natural causes. His brother and successor Ceolwulf I reigned for only two years, but it seems that he carried out the invasion plans already made by his predecessor, because under the year 822 the Welsh Annals describe a twofold disaster for British arms. The fortress of Degannwy in Gwynedd was destroyed by the 'Saxons', who also overran and occupied the neighbouring kingdom of Powys.

Despite William of Malmesbury's dismissive remark that Ceolwulf's reign 'produced nothing worthy', it is clear that Mercia remained a formidable military power. But Ceolwulf was driven from the throne in circumstances which are unknown, and in 823 another distant relative named Beornwulf became king. Perhaps his predecessor had devoted too much attention to a decisive invasion of Wales, and had neglected to secure his power base in Mercia against potential rivals. The sudden disappearance of many of the men who had witnessed charters in Ceolwulf's reign from those of his successor hints at a possible purge of Beornwulf's opponents. One of these ealdormen, Muca, with an otherwise unknown colleague named Burhhelm, was 'killed' in 824, according to an enigmatic entry in the Anglo-Saxon Chronicle.

At any rate Beornwulf displayed considerable energy, and must have seemed a worthy successor to Offa and Coenwulf. He maintained Mercian authority in Kent and Essex, and according to Stenton was 'the dominant figure in southern England as late as the summer of 825'. At that point he decided to invade Wessex; the political background to this invasion is unknown, but the Anglo-Saxon Chronicle records a battle in the same year between Britons and the men of Devon, and Beornwulf may have thought that King Ecgberht was too busy on his western frontier to oppose him. If so, it was a serious miscalculation. The two royal armies clashed at Ellendun, which is usually identified with Wroughton in Wiltshire. Wroughton is only ten miles or so south of Kempsford, the site of the battle of 802, and it is likely that the Mercians had crossed the Thames at the same spot as Aethelmund's Hwicce and were aiming for the same strategic objective, the West Saxon heartland around Winchester. The Chronicle refers to a 'great slaughter', Henry of Huntingdon adding once again that the local stream was choked with corpses and ran red with blood. The Mercians were defeated, and it is probable that, as at the Winwaed, many of their losses occurred when they tried to retreat across the stream, though Beornwulf himself escaped. Ecgberht immediately followed up his triumph by dispatching his son Aethelwulf, with Bishop Ealhstan and Ealdorman Wulfheard, into Kent. Here they drove out a certain Baldred, whom the Chronicle describes as a 'king' but who may have been a viceroy appointed by Beornwulf. The Chronicle, relying as usual on West Saxon sources, claims that the people of Kent and Surrey, with the East and South Saxons, all welcomed Aethelwulf as a liberator, perhaps because they still resented Offa's takeover of 785. Meanwhile the East Angles, 'for fear of the Mercians', also asked for Ecgberht's protection.

The Mercian warrior class had suffered serious losses, but somehow Beornwulf must have raised another army to strike back at his encircling enemies, because later in 825 or 826 he was campaigning on his eastern frontier. His energy was not matched by his luck on the battlefield, however, because the Chronicle concludes with the statement that 'in the same year the East Angles killed Beornwulf, king of the Mercians.' A similar entry for 827 hints at yet another disaster for Mercian arms: 'Here Ludeca, king of Mercia, was killed, and his five ealdormen with him, and Wiglaf succeeded to the kingdom.' Who Ludeca was we are not told, but Florence of Worcester adds that he had led another invasion of East Anglia to avenge Beornwulf's death, and had met an identical fate at the hands of a local army.

154

The 'Bretwaldas'

Wiglaf was not left in peace for long, because under the heading of the year 829 the Anglo-Saxon Chronicle states that Ecgberht 'conquered the kingdom of Mercia and all that was south of the Humber.' At this moment of national triumph for the West Saxons there appears in the Chronicle a passage which has intrigued historians ever since. Ecgberht, it continues, 'was the eighth king who was "Bretwalda"' (alternatively, in some manuscripts, 'Brytenwalda'). This term is generally agreed to mean 'Wide Ruler', or perhaps originally 'Britain Ruler', and it is clearly intended to be the equivalent of what Bede, writing in Latin rather than English, calls 'imperium'. The idea is evidently that up to that date there had been eight English kings whose power had extended beyond their own boundaries and brought most, if not all, of their neighbours into some form of subjection. But, despite the attempts of some scholars to define it more precisely, this cannot have been a formal title or political position with legally defined rights. No one, as far as we know, was ever crowned or acclaimed 'Bretwalda', and it is quite possible that the term was unknown in the lifetimes of most of the men who were said to have earned the distinction. It has been well described as 'a poetic rather than political assertion' (Swanton).

The essential meaninglessness of the title is obvious when the list of the other seven 'Bretwaldas' in the Chronicle is examined. It comprises, in chronological order: King Aelle of the South Saxons (died c. 490), Ceawlin of Wessex (c. 593), Aethelberht of Kent (c. 616), Raedwald of the East Angles (c. 627), and Kings Edwin (616–33), Oswald (634–42) and Oswy (642–70) of Northumbria. It is in fact the same list given by Bede of those kings who had enjoyed the 'imperium' or overlordship of Britain up to his own day. Even then it was highly subjective, for it can hardly be accepted that a migration-era petty king of Sussex, for example, had exercised real power over the entire island. Indeed, by 829 the list was no more than propaganda. If Ecgberht, who had received the temporary submission of the English south of the Humber, merited the title of Bretwalda, how could it have been withheld from Aethelbald, Offa or Coenwulf? Yet not a single Mercian ruler appears in Bede's list or

155

in that of the Chronicle, a fact which alone is sufficient to render them valueless as political documents.

Mercia Eclipsed

After subjugating the new Mercian king, Wiglaf, Ecgberht marched unopposed through Mercia as far as Dore near Sheffield, where he accepted the submission of the Northumbrians. In 830 he was in Wales, where the rulers again offered him tribute, but his triumph proved ephemeral, for the Chronicle entry for the same year says that 'here Wiglaf obtained again the kingdom of Mercia.' As Stenton observes, this is unlikely to have been as a result of Ecgberht's generosity, despite a much later assertion by Roger of Wendover, or the pro-West Saxon Chronicle would have said so. Probably the annal refers to an otherwise undocumented Mercian revolt against the domination of Wessex, which resulted in the heartland of the kingdom quickly reverting to Wiglaf's control. He seems also to have recovered the London area, granting land in Middlesex in a charter of 831, and in 836 he was secure enough to be able to invite the Archbishop of Canterbury to a conference at Croft in Leicestershire. King Aethelstan of East Anglia resumed the minting of his own coins around 830, which suggests that he was also able to take advantage of the Mercian victory to throw off West Saxon rule. Meanwhile Ecgberht's fortunes continued to deteriorate. In 836 he was defeated by the Danes in what the Chronicle admits was a 'great slaughter' in Somerset, and although he routed a combined Cornish and Danish force at Hingston Down in Cornwall in 838, he died a year later.

The locations of Ecgberht's last battles illustrate how, in the first decades of the ninth century, the forays of the Vikings had been diverted away from eastern England towards the north and west. Northumbria had been repeatedly ravaged, but most of the long-ships had sailed around the north of Scotland to pillage and settle the Shetland and Orkney Islands, the Hebrides, the Isle of Man, North Wales and Ireland. Mercia had enjoyed nearly half a century of respite, but this was now coming to an end. In 840 Wiglaf was succeeded by Beorhtwulf, and two years later the Anglo-Saxon Chronicle describes 'a great slaughter in London, in Quentovic, and

156

in Rochester'. Quentovic, situated just across the Straits of Dover, was one of the main commercial centres of the Frankish Empire. Only one agent could have been responsible for this mayhem on both sides of the English Channel, and other Chronicle entries confirm the sense of growing menace as the Vikings tightened their grip on the seas around Western Europe. Later in 842 what was probably the same fleet, having sacked Nantes at the mouth of the River Loire, settled for the winter on the island of Noirmoutier, 'as if they meant to stay for ever', in the words of a Frankish chronicle. This was the first time that a Viking army is recorded as wintering in its southern raiding grounds, but the experiment was successful, as the Franks made no attempt to storm the island stronghold and the raiders were able to resume their operations as soon as the weather improved.

Under the year 850, the Anglo-Saxon Chronicle records the first appearance in England of this sinister new development: although temporarily defeated by a West Saxon army in Devon, 'the heathen men stayed in Thanet over the winter.' At that time it seems that the 'Isle' of Thanet at the north-eastern tip of Kent, where Margate and Ramsgate now stand, was a genuine island, offering the same sort of security against attack as Noirmoutier. King Alfred's biographer Asser, writing half a century later, claims that the raiders' base was Sheppey, a similar island closer to the mouth of the Thames, though the Chronicle dates the first overwintering in Sheppey to four years later. It is of course possible that both places were occupied at different stages of the same campaign.

Kent had remained under West Saxon control and was now permanently outside Beorhtwulf's sphere of influence, but London was still a Mercian city, and was clearly at risk from a Viking fleet based no more than fifty miles to the east. The king responded by raising an army and marching to its defence, but he was too late. In the spring of 851 a Danish fleet, which the Anglo-Saxon Chronicle estimates at 350 ships, sailed into the mouth of the Thames, sent a landing party to sack Canterbury, then descended on London.

At this point it is necessary to confront a longstanding problem in early medieval military history. Is 350 ships a plausible total, and if so how many fighting men does that represent? And more generally, how large were these Viking armies, against which the great powers of Western Europe seemed so helpless? Naturally their victims thought that their numbers were incalculable. The 'Annals of Ulster', for example, describes how 'the sea spewed forth floods of foreigners', so that the country was 'submerged by waves of Vikings and pirates'. This idea was strengthened by the raiders' seaborne mobility, because the same group could attack targets many miles apart in quick succession, giving the impression that there were many such bands operating simultaneously. It has been argued that the smallest ships mentioned in the tenth-century Norwegian 'Leidang', or national levy, had twenty benches for oarsmen, which assuming two men per bench, one rowing on each side, would give a minimum of forty warriors per ship. Other vessels were much bigger – the crew of Olaf Tryggvason's *Long Serpent* at the Battle of Svoldr in the year 1000 has been estimated as over 500 strong (Heath).

However, it is generally agreed that statistics from internal Scandinavian wars, which took place in coastal waters, are not relevant to the long-distance raids of the ninth century, on which the vessels also had to carry supplies and even livestock and could not have risked compromising seaworthiness by overloading. The ship excavated at Gokstad in Norway, believed to date from around the time of the attacks on London, has often been taken as typical of the vessels used in these campaigns. It is seventy-six feet long, built of oak, with sixteen benches each housing a pair of oars. Allowing for a captain, a steersman and a few other supernumeraries, an average figure of thirty-five crewmen per ship would seem reasonable. So if there really were 350 such ships in the fleet which attacked London, it could have carried as many as 10,000 men.

A counterargument has been put forward by P. H. Sawyer, who has claimed that even large Viking armies should be numbered not in thousands, but in hundreds. He reminds us of Ine's dictum that a 'here' or raiding army could be anything from thirty-five men upwards. It is unlikely that any chronicler had the opportunity to count the huge fleets of hundreds of ships mentioned at critical points

158

in the campaigns, and their numbers may have been exaggerated by popular rumour. Even if the count is roughly correct, it might include large numbers of smaller boats, either brought over from Scandinavia as ships' boats or requisitioned locally. And we should remember that the primary method of propulsion of the longships was sail, with oars used mainly in emergencies or for manoeuvring in the confined spaces of rivers and coastal waters. So they could have operated effectively with smaller crews than the number of benches provided would suggest, and may routinely have done so. On the other hand it is possible to overemphasise the small size of Viking armies. If the 260 or more bodies excavated at Repton (see page 169) are really casualties from the Great Army of 874, it was obviously possible for such a force to sustain losses of this magnitude and still remain in the field. A total strength of at least 1,000 can be assumed on this basis, but this was an exceptionally big army, recognised as such by the chroniclers on both sides of the English Channel.

Some explanation other than sheer numbers must nevertheless be sought for the success of the Viking armies in England and elsewhere. Tactically they enjoyed no decisive superiority over the English on land, as is proven by the number of defeats which they suffered. Their armament, in fact, was very similar to that of their Mercian and West Saxon enemies. Mail armour and iron helmets may have been more common among the invaders, but we have no reliable data on the proportion of men on either side who were so equipped, so it is hard to reach a firm conclusion. The long-handled two-handed axes associated with eleventh-century Danes and used by English huscarles on the Bayeux tapestry seem to have been unknown in the ninth century. It has been argued that Viking swords were made of better quality iron than English ones, and their more tapering blades and heavier counterweighted pommels made them better balanced (Loades), but this can only have provided a marginal advantage in the press of a 'shieldwall' fight, though it might have been more useful in individual combat. The Scandinavians made considerable use of the bow, but as has been argued above (page 110) it cannot be proved that the English were

159

not also effective archers. Similarly Viking battlefield formations can be shown to have been fairly sophisticated, at least if the late evidence of Saxo Grammaticus is accepted as relevant, but it is hard to believe that the English, with their long experience of internal wars, were not just as capable.

What the men who attacked Beorhtwulf's London almost certainly did have, however, was a psychological advantage. As seaborne raiders, whose movements were unpredictable and their numbers apparently huge, they would have been frightening enough to the levies of landlocked Mercia; their heathenism and their ferocious attacks on churches and monasteries as well as peaceful settlements must have added to the terror. On the other hand, the invaders would have consisted of the most desperate and warlike elements of their home countries, motivated by the desire to win their fortunes and by the knowledge that defeat so far from their homes was likely to result in their ignominious destruction. They were also largely immune to the logistic problems which the English encountered when raising large armies, and so they did not need to restrict their campaigning to particular seasons. The Vikings did not need supply trains as they were prepared to live off the land, indifferent to the damage this caused to the local economy, and in any case their ships were available to store and transport their loot. Paradoxically for such relentless aggressors, the one strategy which the invaders used time and again, and which their enemies found almost impossible to counter, was a defensive one. They would retire across the sea, or into fortified camps on islands, and then return to the attack when their enemies least expected them.

The notice in the Anglo-Saxon Chronicle is as usual too brief to reconstruct Beorhtwulf's 851 campaign in detail, but his army evidently attacked the enemy somewhere in the London area north of the Thames, only to be 'put to flight'. This implies that the Mercians did not put up much resistance, but subsequent events show that they had fought hard enough to divert the Vikings south-wards, and quite possibly to weaken them seriously. The Chronicle goes on to record that the Danish army crossed the Thames into Surrey, where King Aethelwulf of Wessex and his son Aethelbald brought them to battle at a place known as Aclea. The site has not been certainly identified but was probably at Ockley, six miles south of Dorking. Here the West Saxons gained the victory, and in the words of the Chronicle 'made the greatest slaughter of a heathen raiding army that we have ever heard tell of.' The same entry records a perhaps even more significant development, for the West Saxons and their Kentish allies were now learning to take the fight to the enemy at sea: 'And the same year King Athelstan [another son of Aethelwulf, and his viceroy in Kent] and ealdorman Ealhhere fought in ships, and struck a great raiding army at Sandwich, and captured nine ships and put the others to flight.'

This series of events seems to have marked a decisive turning point for Mercia. As well as defeat at the hands of the Vikings, the kingdom was being torn apart by internal faction fighting. In 849, according to the later 'Life of Saint Wigstan' (Jennings), Wigstan, a grandson of Wiglaf and so presumably a rival for the throne, was assassinated by Beorhtwulf's son Beorhtfrith at a council meeting, along with three of his companions. Beorhtfrith had until then been the heir apparent, but he disappears from the sources thereafter, perhaps exiled by his father for the murder. Around that time the area which is now Berkshire passed – apparently peacefully – under West Saxon control, though its Mercian ealdorman, another Aethelwulf, retained his position. Beorhtwulf continued to undertake aggressive campaigns in Wales, and his troops were presumably the 'Saxons' whom the Welsh Annals record as killing King Meurig of Gwent, also in 849.

After Beorhtwulf's death in 852 the kingdom adopted an increasingly subordinate role to the rising power of the West Saxons. The Anglo-Saxon Chronicle records how in the following year his successor, an ealdorman named Burhred, asked King Aethelwulf for help in subduing the Welsh, who had obviously tried to throw off their allegiance in the wake of the Mercian succession crisis. The army of Wessex marched through Mercia, and together the allies managed to restore Burhred's authority among the Welsh kingdoms. Asser reports that Aethelwulf then returned home – but for a Mercian king to require West Saxon help to restore order in his own back yard was a new and worrying phenomenon. The alliance was cemented immediately afterwards by Burhred's marriage to Aethelwulf's daughter Aethelswith – celebrated, says Asser, at the West Saxon royal estate of Chippenham.

From this time onwards Mercia has often been seen as a mere vassal of the West Saxon kings, reversing the position of Offa's reign, but there is evidence that the kingdom remained genuinely independent, even though the alliance with Wessex had come to dominate its foreign policy. In 865 the Mercians attacked Gwynedd without West Saxon help, advancing successfully as far as Anglesey, and when, at around the same time, the coinage of the two countries was standardised, it was Burhred's designs which were adopted in Wessex (G. Williams, in Brown and Farr).

The same year, however, saw the beginning of a new and infinitely more serious threat from across the sea. The Danes had been temporarily diverted from south-east England by their defeat at Aclea, but they and their Norwegian cousins continued to prowl around the coast of Britain, striking wherever opposition was weak and on occasion penetrating far inland. One of Burhred's charters refers to events in 855, when 'pagans' were in the country of the Wreocensetan, around the Wrekin in present-day Shropshire. This area is fifty miles from the open sea, and that the Vikings could appear even there indicates that few regions even of inland Mercia were entirely safe. It is likely that this was the same raiding army that attacked North Wales in 856 and was destroyed on Anglesey by Rhodri ap Merfyn, otherwise known as 'Rhodri the Great', the king of Gwynedd. In 860 a great raid from the sea destroyed Winchester, before being defeated by the men of Hampshire and the former Mercian province of Berkshire under their ealdormen Osric and Aethelwulf. But in 865 the enemy finally arrived to stay.

The Great Army
The 'heathen raiding army' which, according to the Anglo-Saxon Chronicle, stayed in Thanet over the winter of 865 may not necessarily have been much larger than those involved in previous invasions, but it introduced an ominous new development. The Vikings made

peace with the people of Kent in exchange for payment – the first record in England of the notorious 'Danegeld' – then ignored the agreement and plundered eastern Kent regardless. Later in the year, either this or another army then landed in East Anglia, whose rulers had obtained their independence from Mercia but had never recovered their former strength. Again the invaders made peace with the ineffectual King Edmund, and settled down to spend the winter, no longer bothering to find a defensible island off the coast for their base. In fact, far from fighting back, the East Angles seem to have actively colluded with them. In the spring they provided them with horses, and as soon as the harvest was in, what was to become known to history as the 'Micel Here' or 'Great Army' rode away northwards. Their target was Northumbria, which had long ago lost its position as the foremost military power in England, and which was currently being further weakened by a civil war over succession. It is likely that Edmund had carefully briefed the Vikings on his neighbour's problems in the hope of encouraging them to move on – a policy which was spectacularly successful, though only in the short term.

An eleventh-century version of the Anglo-Saxon Chronicle names the leaders of the Great Army as Ingware, Halfdan and Ubbi, who, it is implied, were brothers. If three brothers did indeed share the command it could explain the remarkable flexibility of this army, which on several occasions split into separate divisions and then reformed for major offensives. Scandinavian legend claimed that they were the sons of Ragnar, one of the leaders of the attacks on France in the 840s and 850s, and sometimes identified with the semi-mythical hero Ragnar Lothbrock. Ragnar was said to have gone raiding around York and been captured by King Aelle, who put him to death by having him thrown into a pit filled with poisonous snakes. His sons were now keen to avenge him, although as a motive for the invasion of Northumbria this story hardly seems convincing. It has been pointed out that if Ragnar had done all the deeds attributed to him he must have been well over 100 years old by the time Aelle came to the throne (Jones). And the only British venomous snake, the northern adder, is not particularly dangerous or aggressive. Its bite very occasionally kills a child, but as a method of murdering a full-grown Viking it would not be very reliable.

Ingware, also known as Ivar the Boneless, also seems at first sight to belong more to legend than to history. According to Scandinavian legend he was born without a skeleton, with only gristle instead of bones. Some researchers believe that this bizarre story indicates that Ivar suffered from a known hereditary disease, osteogenesis imperfecta, which would have seriously disabled him physically but left his mental abilities unaffected (Sykes). He may of course have been thought to have supernatural powers, but that someone with such a disability could survive to adulthood and attain command of an army suggests that Viking society was more compassionate than we might expect. However, the evidence for Ivar's condition is far from conclusive, and one remark quoted in its favour – that he was carried aloft on a shield – might refer to a triumphal celebration of victory rather than implying that he was unable to walk.

Late in 866 the Great Army moved north to York, whether in search of revenge or simply for loot. The Anglo-Saxon Chronicle says that it crossed the estuary of the Humber, which suggests that the Danes were travelling at least part of the way by ship, although any parties going overland must have traversed the Mercian province of Lindsey on the way, apparently without meeting any opposition. The Northumbrian king Osberht had recently been driven from the throne by the usurper Aelle, who, according to Asser, did not belong to the royal family and so was not universally accepted. In the chaos the Vikings were able to occupy York before either of the rival kings became aware of their arrival, and it was not until the following spring that Osberht and Aelle agreed to make a truce and combine their forces to attack them.

On or about Palm Sunday, 23 March, the Northumbrians forced their way into the city. Asser says that this was possible because York lacked proper walls, which is an interesting statement because it had been securely walled in Roman times. Despite York's political and religious importance, and its strategic position on the main route from the south into the Northumbrian heartland, its rulers had not thought it worthwhile to maintain its defences. The Anglo-Saxon

Chronicle describes a ferocious battle in the streets as the Vikings rallied and counterattacked. Those Northumbrians who had entered the city were trapped and slaughtered, so probably the crumbling Roman walls were still enough of an obstacle to slow them down as they fled. The fight then continued outside York, as the defenders sallied out and attacked the English troops who had remained behind. Both the rival kings and eight of their ealdormen were killed, and the Northumbrians suffered a catastrophic defeat. The survivors, we are told, 'made peace'. Among them was an obscure thegn called Egbert, whom the Danish brothers appointed as a puppet king before they embarked on a summer of plundering throughout the kingdom as far north as the River Tyne. York seems to have been occupied as a more or less permanent base for the raiders. One of England's oldest and most prestigious kingdoms had been effectively destroyed in a single day's fighting.

How Burhred regarded the destruction of Mercia's most ancient rival from a political point of view we do not know, but he seems not to have grasped the strategic lesson of the York campaign. Sixty miles south of York was the town of Nottingham, which guarded the Mercian end of the same north–south route which had been the site of so many battles in the past. Nottingham was a smaller town, but it was a naturally defensible site on high ground overlooking the River Trent. Nevertheless it appears to have been left ungarrisoned, and in 867 the Great Army advanced south and occupied it un-opposed. We are not told whether they came by ship via the Rivers Humber and Trent, as seems likely, or whether the horses obtained from the East Angles were pressed into service for an overland march, but in either case the move could have been completed in three or four days, far too quickly for Burhred to react in time to intercept them. Instead the Vikings were allowed to settle into winter quarters while the Mercian king appealed to Wessex for help. In the spring a West Saxon army entered Mercia and marched north in company with Burhred's own forces. It was led by King Aethelred of Wessex and his brother Alfred, who was soon to achieve fame as king in his own right.

165

According to the Chronicle the allies besieged the Danes in their 'fortification', but there was no serious fighting and 'the Mercians made peace with the raiding army.' Asser adds that the 'pagans' refused to come out and fight, and the English 'could not break the wall.' Ian Walker has suggested that it was the West Saxons who abandoned the campaign first, giving rise to resentment in Mercia and weakening their alliance, but our admittedly pro-West Saxon sources do not say this. Probably the Vikings were hoping that the besiegers would weaken themselves by a rash assault on the defences and lay themselves open to a counterattack as the Northumbrians had done, but the English refused to oblige them.

In fact, despite the humiliating implications which were becoming attached to 'making peace' with the invaders, it seems that this confrontation was a Mercian victory of sorts. The Vikings returned to York, and did not launch another major attack on Mercia for four years. They could not, of course, remain idle for long, because they still constituted a predatory army which had to live off the land and so were obliged to find new sources of supplies and loot when their neighbourhood was exhausted. After a quiet year on the defensive they returned to East Anglia in 870 under the joint command of Ivar and Ubbi. Again crossing Mercian territory apparently without trouble, they wintered near Thetford.

This move is of interest because it could not have made use of any major waterways and so must have been carried out on horseback. The choice of Thetford suggests that the Danes had by now become virtually independent of their fleet. King Edmund this time refused to negotiate, but instead mustered an army and attacked them. Abbo of Fleury, writing in the late tenth century, says that the encounter took place at a site called Haegelisdun, which is unidentified, but based on the similarity of the place names may have been at Hellesdon near Norwich. Possibly Edmund played into the enemy's hands by assaulting a fortified camp. The Chronicle simply reports that he was killed, and in the aftermath his whole country was conquered by the Danes. The king was buried at Beadoriceswyrthe, later to become known as Bury Saint Edmunds, and before the end of the century his remains had become the focus of a Christian cult (Stenton). This suggests that there may be some truth in the legend that he was taken alive by the Vikings and later murdered by being shot with arrows. At about the same time the monastery at Peterborough was destroyed, and all the abbots and monks allegedly slaughtered.

After that the Great Army moved into Wessex and occupied Reading. This was part of the formerly Mercian territory of Berkshire taken over around 849, and its ealdorman Aethelwulf was still in control after more than twenty years. The Chronicle records that he met the invaders at a place which was to become known as Englefield, some six miles west of Reading between the Rivers Bourne and Kennet. Asser confirms that the name means 'Field of the Angles', commemorating the Mercian ealdorman and his followers who defeated the Danes and drove them back into the town of Reading. Four days later, however, the victorious Angles joined their West Saxon allies under King Aethelred and Alfred and assaulted the town, with predictable results. Although they could sometimes beat the Vikings in the open field, the English had yet to devise a method of capturing their defended strongholds. The Wessex army was defeated in 'a great slaughter', and among the dead was the Mercian veteran Aethelwulf. Four days after that was fought the most famous battle of the war, at Ashdown, where Alfred led an uphill charge against the Danes while the king was still hearing mass, and the invaders were put to flight with 'thousands' killed. The bloody struggle continued along the Berkshire and Wiltshire Downs throughout the spring of 871, with both sides claiming victories but neither able to strike a decisive blow.

Aethelred died after Easter 871, whether by violence or not is not known, and Alfred succeeded to the throne of Wessex. After the death of Aethelwulf the Mercians seem to have taken no part in the campaign, but in May the West Saxons were beaten at Wilton and an exhausted Alfred made peace, probably by offering tribute. During this campaign the Danes had been reinforced by the arrival of what the Chronicle calls a 'summer fleet', consisting of men who intended to stay only for the summer raiding season and then return to their homelands. This is one of several such reinforcements

167

mentioned in the sources, and it is likely that the core of the Great Army which went into winter quarters in England was greatly strengthened every summer by adventurers who retained their farms in Scandinavia and had no intention of settling permanently.

Probably eastern Wessex was too badly ravaged to support the Great Army any longer even if its leaders had not agreed to a cessation of hostilities. At the end of 871 they moved back into Mercian territory and occupied London, once again apparently unopposed. The Mercians also, in the words of the Chronicle, 'made peace.' This time there seems no doubt that Burhred had bought them off. A document survives from the following year recording the sale of a lease of some land at Nuthurst in Warwickshire by Bishop Waerferth of the Hwicce. In it the bishop remarks that he is only agreeing to the sale because of 'the immense tribute of the barbarians, in that same year when the pagans stayed in London' – in other words he needed the gold to pay his share of the Danegeld.

Two aspects of this situation are especially puzzling. One is Burhred's apparent cowardice, twice making peace without putting up serious resistance, in contrast to the ferocious resistance conducted in Wessex by Aethelred and Alfred. The other is the contrasting fates of the four English kingdoms which had still been independent in 865. Two of them, Northumbria and East Anglia, had been effectively destroyed, each as a result of a single battle. Wessex, on the other hand, had taken terrible punishment in years of fighting, but was still able to raise new armies and continue the struggle. Mercia, meanwhile, had hardly been touched. Apart from the obvious prize of London, and the half-hearted sortie to Nottingham, the Vikings had consistently skirted round the kingdom, making no attempt to strike at its heart. Was Burhred actually a more formidable opponent than the Wessex-based Chronicle makes him appear? If their past history was not enough, the victory at Englefield, acknowledged even by the West Saxons, shows that the Angles still knew how to fight.

According to Roger of Wendover, in 872 a group of Northumbrians rebelled against the puppet king Egbert and took refuge in Mercia, where Burhred gave them asylum. The next year saw the Great

Army move its headquarters from London to Torksey, on the lower Trent in Lincolnshire. This was a classic Viking base, on a navigable river, protected by marshes and situated in the midst of rich and so far unravaged agricultural land. It was at least nominally still part of Burhred's kingdom, but no clashes with the Mercians are recorded. Then in the following spring, 874, the Vikings made a swift and obviously unexpected move. Sailing and rowing up the Trent, they descended suddenly on Repton, at the very core of ancient Mercia and the traditional resting place of its kings. Once again Burhred seemed incapable of organising resistance, but this symbolic blow to the heart of the kingdom appears to have broken his will and discredited him in the eyes of his supporters. The king, who had reigned for twenty-two years, hastily fled the country and went to live in Rome, where he subsequently died. A certain Ceolwulf, whom the Anglo-Saxon Chronicle famously dismisses as 'a foolish king's thegn', took over the throne as a vassal of the Danes, being forced to swear humiliatingly that the country 'should be ready for them whichever day they might want it.' It seemed that after all Mercia was another hollow shell of a kingdom which could be shattered by a single blow like East Anglia and Northumbria, and this time without even a lost battle to salvage its honour.

Excavations at Repton undertaken between 1974 and 1988 revealed a surprising amount of information about the brief Viking occupation of 874 and 875 (Biddle and Kjolbye-Biddle). A 'D'-shaped defensive earthwork was found on the south bank of the Trent, into which the vandalised ruins of the stone church of Saint Wystan had been incorporated as a sort of strongpoint. This building was already an important minster church in the eighth and ninth centuries, and contained a mausoleum which housed the remains of several Mercian kings, including Aethelbald and Wiglaf. Its irreverent treatment by the pagan invaders must have been seen by most Mercians as a desecration. Several burials identified as Viking were found around the church, at least one of which was of a woman. Outside the earthwork, but identifiable by coin finds as dating from the same period, was a mass burial of approximately 260 bodies in what had probably been an Anglo-Saxon stone crypt, four-fifths of which

169

were of males between 15 and 45 years old. The excavators believed that it was possible to identify skeletal features similar to those characteristic of Scandinavia, but this sort of analysis is very subjective. Perhaps more reliable is their description of them as 'massively robust', which obviously suggests a group of well-fed and physically fit warriors, although in that case the lack of obvious battle injuries on the bones seems strange.

The site had been opened in the late seventeenth century, when it was reported that in the centre of the mass burial was a coffin containing a human body nine feet long, but unfortunately no trace of this Viking giant was found during the latest excavation. The presence of four pits outside the building, but apparently contemporary and containing individual bodies, hints at human sacrifice and argues against the alternative explanation that the main burial was of monks from the nearby monastery, who might be just as robust as soldiers as a result of an unusually good diet. The excavators suggested that the mass burial did not necessarily mean that there had been a serious mortality in the camp, but that the bodies of members of the Great Army who died at Repton and elsewhere may have been collected and reinterred to accompany the deceased king who must have been in the lost coffin. In that case the implication of the lack of battle injuries is that the Vikings had lost at least as many men to disease, and perhaps hunger, as they had to enemy action. However, it has recently been suggested that the bones, many of which were already disarticulated when they were placed in the grave, might have been supplemented by remains collected from the local cemetery and rearranged, for some inscrutable reason, around the central burial (Fleming). At the same time another cemetery, established within sight of the damaged church, was the site of more-traditional Viking cremation burials.

The Danes did not immediately follow up their advantage after the seizure of Repton, but instead dispersed in several directions. Halfdan returned to Northumbria, where he established a base on the River Tyne and raided the Picts and the Britons of Strathclyde. Then, in 876, the Chronicle reports that he divided up the land among his followers and set them to ploughing and 'providing for

170

themselves'. This seems a surprising change of policy for a Viking, but it appears likely that the objective of the Great Army had always been land for settlement. The presence of non-combatants in the cemetery at Repton suggests that many of the warriors had already brought over their families or acquired new ones in England, and after a decade of overwintering there the ties of the original veterans to their homelands must have been considerably weakened. The three 'kings' Guthrum, Oscytel and Anund went to the borders of East Anglia and encamped at Cambridge, while others continued the fight against Wessex.

At harvest time in the year 877, we are told that the 'raiding army' returned to Mercia, divided part of the country among themselves, and 'gave' the remainder to King Ceolwulf. The timing suggests a certain ruthless acquisitiveness among the Vikings: probably they intended to seize at least some of the harvest which had been sown, and perhaps even already gathered, by Mercian farmers on the land they took from them. English families may have been evicted in places, and left to starve while the invaders enjoyed the fields and barns full of grain. But the Chronicle's description is not one of a military operation, and there is no hint that the local inhabitants or their leaders offered any resistance. This contrasts with the situation in Wessex, where, under the year 871, the Chronicle notes that, in addition to the campaigns undertaken by the king and his ealdor-men and thegns, there were no fewer than nine 'folcgefeoht', or 'people's fights' against the invaders, which must surely imply spontaneous local resistance movements. This strange acquiescence was not because the Mercian army had ceased to exist. In 878 the Welsh Annals record that the formidable King Rhodri of Gwynedd and his son Gwriad were killed by invading 'Saxons', who can only be Ceolwulf's forces. And even in the following decade Asser states that many of the Welsh came to seek West Saxon protection against the continuing 'tyranny' of the Mercians.

In midwinter 878 Guthrum's Danish forces in the south, having made peace with Wessex, broke their agreement and launched a sudden attack on Alfred's base at Chippenham. The West Saxons were taken by surprise and scattered, and the Chronicle reports that many of them fled overseas. The whole country was overrun, but the king himself and a few companions escaped into the forests of Somerset. From there Alfred began the epic struggle to reclaim his kingdom, which was ultimately to bring not just Wessex but the whole of England under the rule of his dynasty.

There are obvious parallels between the surprise attacks on Chippenham and Repton, and it would not be surprising that the Great Army's leaders would seek to repeat a tactic that had been so successful on a previous occasion. It is possible that the dramatic difference between the West Saxon and Mercian experiences of Viking conquest was due mainly to the fact that Alfred survived his defeat and exile, whereas Burhred, who may also have intended to make a comeback after the disaster at Repton, was unfortunate enough to die before he could put his plans into action. This seems unlikely, however, as there is other evidence that the relations between the Danes and the Angles were fundamentally different from those with the Saxons.

This is a priori quite plausible, because Angeln was situated very close to the southern borders of Denmark, and the two peoples and their languages were closely related. As discussed in Chapter 2, most of the inhabitants of the 'Anglian' kingdoms were probably not actually descended from recent immigrants, but culturally they clearly believed themselves to be of the same stock. Place name evidence gives a fairly clear picture of the areas where the Great Army and subsequent Danish immigrants settled. Although not stated in the Anglo-Saxon Chronicle, it is obvious that the portion of Mercia which they divided up and farmed was in the north and east, roughly north of a line running from Stafford to London. Further north Danish names are found throughout Lincolnshire and Yorkshire, and in East Anglia. (The Scandinavian settlements in Cumbria, west of the Pennines, seem to have been mainly Norwegian in origin, and although roughly contemporary they were not a result of the Great Army's campaign.)

For a time in the early tenth century this line of demarcation was recognised by the kings of Wessex, and later England, and the land beyond it became known as the Danelaw. It has been noted,

172

however, that although Essex, the home of the East Saxons, was on the Danish side of the frontier, it was never colonised by Danish settlers. It seems as if the Danes only put down roots in areas whose native population was Anglian – although they were happy to plunder the Saxons they never saw them as potential neighbours (Oppenheimer). The logical conclusion is that relations between the newcomers and the population of the Mercian heartland were not necessarily unfriendly. Of course foraging armies are never likely to be popular with their hosts, but in an age in which population densities were relatively low there was probably room to accommodate a few thousand farmers without having to dispossess the existing occupants of the land.

Place name evidence from Lincolnshire and neighbouring counties has suggested that names ending in the suffix '-by' – a strong indicator of Danish settlement – are concentrated on light, sandy soil on the upper reaches of tributaries rather than on the fertile ground beside the main rivers. Possibly the Danes preferred these areas as reminiscent of conditions in Denmark, but it also seems likely that they were reluctant to dispossess their Anglian neighbours en masse, or simply lacked the strength to do so (Wood, 1986). The plundering activities of the previous few years had probably fallen heaviest on the rich and undefended monastic estates such as Peterborough, which greatly agitated the chroniclers, but which the ordinary Anglian peasant might not have perceived as a personal threat. Our sources constantly emphasise the distinction between Christians and 'pagans', but even this may not have been the barrier it seems. J. D. Richards has interpreted the two cemeteries at Repton as evidence of open rivalry between Christian and pagan elements, and suggested that Halfdan's men, who had by then lived in England for nearly ten years, were already in the process of conversion by 874, while the more recent arrivals under Guthrum were still pagan. The latter might have set up their cremation site within sight of the church at Repton as a deliberate challenge to the foreign influences that were affecting, and in their eyes corrupting, their comrades.

So was the Viking objective in their attacks on Mercia mainly dynastic? Was their quarrel not with the people but with King Burhred personally? Was Ceolwulf purely a Danish puppet, or a popular candidate for the throne who followed the common practice of inviting a neighbouring power to assist him? And was the division of the land really a version of 'ethnic cleansing' at the expense of the general population, a welcome addition to the man-power of the kingdom, or a negotiated reward to Ceolwulf's allies for their help against Burhred? In the latter case the new king seems to have miscalculated, because the Danes were not at all keen to accept English overlordship and a long struggle for supremacy lay ahead. Perhaps that is why the Chronicle describes him as 'foolish', rather than treacherous, cowardly, or any of the other insulting epithets which might have come to mind.

It is not clear what happened to Ceolwulf, but his reign was apparently short. According to an eleventh-century king list he held the throne for five years, and it is possible that his death is implied in a laconic entry in the Welsh Annals for 880 describing a battle at Conway: 'vengeance for Rhodri at God's hand'. William of Malmesbury's epitaph for Ceolwulf, which concludes his chapter on the Mercian kings, is characteristically brutal: 'Thus the sovereignty of the Mercians, which prematurely bloomed by the overweening ambition of a heathen [i.e. Penda], altogether withered away through the inactivity of a driveller king, in the year of our Lord's incarnation eight hundred and seventy five.'

Chapter 10

The 'Liberation' and the Triumph of Wessex

At any rate, Ceolwulf II was the last generally acknowledged king of Mercia, his death bringing to an end the dynasty which had ruled the heart of England for nearly three centuries. The next surviving record of events is a charter of 883 which was issued by Aethelred, 'ealdorman of the Mercians', with the approval of 'King Alfred and the whole Mercian council'. The last few years had seen a dramatic change in the fortunes of the West Saxons and their leader. In the summer of 878 he emerged from his refuge, mustered the fighting men of Somerset, Wiltshire and Hampshire, and inflicted a decisive defeat on the Danes at the Battle of Ethandune on the slopes of the Wiltshire Downs. Guthrum, driven into his camp and besieged there for a fortnight, surrendered and agreed to be baptised. A formal peace was made at Wedmore, and the invaders retired to settle on the land in East Anglia.

For the next few years the Anglo-Saxon Chronicle records Viking raids against the Franks, and a minor engagement at sea in which four shiploads of renegade Danes were defeated by Alfred's fleet, but on the whole England was left in peace. It is not clear who ealdorman Aethelred was: he was probably a native Mercian, but he owed his position to Alfred and obviously recognised him as his overlord. The two men may well have developed a relationship based on mutual respect, for they were both outstanding war leaders. In a later charter Aethelred is described as 'dux et patricius',

175

'earl and patrician', of Mercia, but he never took the title of king, though Aethelweard's version of the Chronicle does use it to describe him, probably anachronistically.

In 885 a raiding army from France broke the peace when it attacked Rochester, but Alfred repulsed it and retaliated by a seaborne raid on East Anglia. In the following year he recaptured London from the Viking force which had occupied it since 879, repaired the physical damage done by their occupation, and then handed it over to Aethelred to govern on his behalf. Another treaty with Guthrum formalised relations with what had now become recognised as a separate Danish kingdom in the east of England. At about the same time Aethelred married Alfred's daughter Aethelflaed, later to become famous as the 'Lady of the Mercians'. Asser tells us that 'all the Angles and Saxons' not under Viking rule 'turned willingly to King Alfred and submitted themselves to his lordship.' This is not unlikely, as Alfred was the only English leader who seemed to be able to offer protection against the invaders. Nevertheless, if the Mercians were now junior partners in the alliance, they still had an important part to play. Aethelred was still in control of more than half of the territory of Offa's kingdom south and west of the Danelaw, and to judge from the charters which he continued to issue he was allowed a large degree of autonomy. He also campaigned independently in South Wales, causing the Welsh rulers to protest to Alfred about his 'tyrannical behaviour'.

In 892 another great Danish army arrived in Kent in 250 ships, later supplemented by another eighty under Haesten. Guthrum had by now died, and the Danes of East Anglia, under his successor Eric, launched raids of their own to take advantage of the confusion. Most of the fighting in this campaign occurred in south-east England, where the West Saxon armies, probably with the aid of Mercian reinforcements, had the best of it. They defeated a Danish army at Farnham and forced it to abandon all its loot and escape across the Thames at a place where there was no ford, which must have led to further losses of equipment if not loss of life from drowning. They subsequently stormed Haesten's camp at Benfleet, burned his fleet and took his wife and children hostage. This success was possible because the main Danish force was absent from its base at the time, but is significant because it was the first time that an English army had taken a fortified Viking camp by assault. Haesten's family were returned to him as a gesture of reconciliation, and because his sons were the god-children of Alfred and Aethelred, but this did not bring about peace.

Instead Haesten led a great raiding army against Mercia. Why this region was targeted we do not know, but it implies that the Danes were well aware of the Mercian role in their defeats. They managed to make their way, by a route which is unclear, from the Thames to the mouth of the Severn, and up that river into western Mercia. The Anglo-Saxon Chronicle describes the Vikings going 'up the Thames until they reached the Severn', but as there is no passage by water from the upper reaches of the Thames into the Severn it seems likely that they took the sea route along the south coast of England and round Land's End. They were reinforced by raiders from East Anglia and Northumbria, although the Chronicle does not make it clear whether these were all Danes, or whether some of their English subjects also joined them, glad of an opportunity to avenge themselves on the Mercians who had once dominated them. Alfred was busy campaigning in Devon, but Aethelred, with the West Saxon ealdormen Aethelhelm and Aethelnoth, gathered an army to resist the invasion, mustering men not only from all over southern England, but even some allies from North Wales. They went in pursuit of the Vikings, probably on horseback, and caught them at a place called Buttington, which has been identified either with a site near the confluence of the Rivers Severn and Wye, or more credibly further upstream at the village of Buttington near Welshpool, where traces of an earthwork of possibly Anglo-Saxon date still survive (Swanton (trans.), *Anglo-Saxon Chronicle*, 1996).

The Danes built a defensive camp and Aethelred invested it from all sides, deploying his troops on both sides of the river. Eventually the besieged Danes ran out of food; when they had eaten their horses and were on the verge of starvation they sallied out and attacked the English on the eastern bank. The Chronicle says that many Englishmen of rank were killed, singling out a king's thegn named Ordhere for special mention, but the Danes were defeated with 'great slaughter'. The survivors retired to their ships and fled back to Essex, only to regroup and sail back round the coast, this time landing near Chester. They occupied the town before the English could catch them; strangely the Chronicle calls it 'deserted', perhaps meaning that most of the houses were outside the old Roman walls, which were consequently undefended.

Aethelred's troops were again mounted on horses, but they were not equipped for an assault on a fortified town. They contented themselves with ravaging the countryside and bottling up the Vikings inside the defences, one of the less glamorous aspects of warfare which is graphically described in the Chronicle: they 'took all the cattle that were outside there, and killed all the men they could ride down outside the fort; and burned up all the corn, and with their horses ate up all the neighbourhood.' Once again deprived of supplies, the invaders abandoned Chester and retreated into Wales, from where they finally sailed home to East Anglia for the winter.

Fighting resumed in the south in the 894 season, and in the following year Alfred succeeded in bottling up the Danes in their stronghold on the River Lea, twenty miles above London. He built two forts of his own on either side of the river and blocked the channel between them, so that the enemy could not get their ships out. They therefore broke out overland and struck out north-westwards across Mercia to Bridgnorth on the Severn, where the name implies that there was already a bridge by which they could cross the river. This time no attempt seems to have been made to bring them to bay, although the Chronicle records that part of Alfred's army – perhaps the men of Mercia under Aethelred – followed them while the rest remained behind to capture the Danish fleet and take the still-serviceable ships into London. Probably both sides were exhausted by this time, and the invaders were apparently allowed to stay at Bridgnorth unmolested until they dispersed of their own accord in the spring of 896. The crisis was over, and although fighting continued on a smaller scale, the Anglo-Saxon Chronicle was perhaps justified in playing down the threat presented by this latest 'Great Army'. The entry for the year 896 remarks that, 'by the grace of God', the English had not been crushed, and had in fact suffered worse over the previous few years from human and cattle diseases and from the deaths of a number of leading ealdormen and thegns, apparently not by enemy action.

King Alfred died in October 899, and was succeeded by his son Edward. However, the new king had a rival, his cousin Aethelwold, who made a bungled attempt to seize the throne. Edward cornered him at the royal manor of Wimborne in Dorset, but he escaped north to Northumbria and collected a motley following of Vikings and dissident Englishmen to support his bid for power. In 903 he launched a great raid on Mercia in alliance with the Danes of East Anglia under King Eric. Edward mustered an army containing contingents from Wessex, Kent and probably Mercia as well, and went in pursuit. He was apparently unable to catch them, however, before they reached safety in East Anglia, because the Chronicle records that he retaliated by devastating their country as far north as the Fens. In order to carry out this sort of 'scorched earth' strategy it was necessary to disperse his forces, but Edward was insistent that the army should regroup and return to Mercia in a single body in order to reduce the risk of being overrun by pursuing Danes. The men from Kent failed to rejoin him, though, despite receiving seven messengers ordering them to do so, and paid the price when a Danish army caught up and surrounded them. The site of this battle was at Holme, probably identifiable with the village of that name a few miles south of Peterborough, on the edge of the Fen marshes. Edward turned back and may have surrounded the Danes in their turn, which would explain the extraordinary death toll in this fight, as neither side would have been able to retreat. The Chronicle lists six leading men who were killed on the English side, and says that the Vikings remained in possession of the field, but as Edward was carrying out a planned retirement this need not indicate that he was defeated. Among the Danes and their allies the dead included King Eric, the pretender Aethelwold and 'very many others'.

With all their leaders dead, the Danes of East Anglia had no choice but to make peace with Edward, although the Viking attacks were by no means over. In 910 the Anglo-Saxon Chronicle states that the 'barbarians' of Northumbria 'broke the peace', though it is likely that their action was a reprisal for an attack by Edward and Aethelred on Lindsey in the previous year. During this campaign the Mercians brought the much-travelled body of Saint Oswald from Bardney – where it had rested since Queen Osthryth took it there two centuries earlier – and installed it at Gloucester. It would not be surprising if this action had upset the English Northumbrians as well as the Danes, and Aethelweard's version of the Chronicle says that the invasion of 910 was specifically aimed at Aethelred as much as at the West Saxon king. The Chronicle is confused at this point, and what is obviously the same battle is listed three times under different years, but Aethelweard's is the most detailed account and probably, because of its Mercian perspective, the most reliable.

The raiders cut a swathe of destruction through northern Mercia, crossed the Severn at Bridgnorth and plundered the country to the west, then turned for home, 'rejoicing in rich spoil'. They were intercepted on 5 August 910 by a combined Mercian and West Saxon army which was apparently under the command of Aethelred, since King Edward was not present. The exact site of the ensuing battle is uncertain: Aethelweard gives it as Woden's Field, presumably Wednesfield, east of Wolverhampton, but other versions of the Chronicle mention Tettenhall, about four miles further west. It may in fact have been a running fight with clashes at both places, since Aethelweard states that the English attacked while the enemy were still crossing the Severn at Bridgnorth, which is ten miles west of Tettenhall and even further from Wednesfield. It seems likely that the Danes were attacked successively from both directions and harried eastwards from the bridge, until they were stopped by an English division which 'had got in front of the raiding army' and blocked its retreat.

Aethelweard's 'great victory on Woden's Field' may then have been the culmination of a desperate attempt by the Danes to break out of a developing encirclement. It failed, and the invaders were defeated with heavy loss. Three Viking kings, Halfdan, Eowils and

Ivar, as well as numerous 'jarls' and other noblemen, were among those who the Chronicle says were sent hastening to hell. This triumph was Aethelred's last battle, because the following year he died and was buried in his stronghold at Gloucester. It has been suggested, on the basis of a later mention of his ill health in an Irish annal, that he may have died from wounds received at Tettenhall (Walker), but there is no real evidence for this, and in view of the fact that he had been ruling Mercia for around thirty years he may have been of fairly advanced age.

The Lady of the Mercians

Aethelred had left no male heir, but his widow Aethelflaed seems to have taken on the role of leader of the Mercians without opposition. This was unusual, because no woman seems ever to have ruled an Anglo-Saxon kingdom before, or even to have been considered for the role. But the circumstances were also unusual. Firstly, although often regarded as 'the last ruler of an independent Mercia', she was not a crowned queen, but retained her husband's rather ambivalent position as a 'sub king' or viceroy under the ultimate authority of the king of Wessex. Also, her position as the sister of this king and the daughter of Alfred the Great gave her a personal prestige which few other women could have enjoyed. The Mercians seem always to have allowed women greater influence in public life than was customary in Wessex, perhaps because of the number of different male lines competing for the throne. The support of other powerful families was obtained through marriage alliances, which naturally gave the women concerned more influence than would have been the case if the king owed his position to his own family alone. It has been pointed out that the wives of Offa, Wiglaf, Beorhtwulf and Burhred all routinely witnessed their husbands' charters, and that Offa even issued coins featuring the image of Queen Cynefrith, a unique phenomenon for the Anglo-Saxon period. It is also of course necessary to acknowledge the importance of personal qualities. In 911 Aethelflaed already had a long history of supporting her husband in the government of Mercia under the most difficult circumstances, and both King Edward and the Mercian nobility must have been aware of her exceptional ability. Leaving aside whatever prejudices some may have had, she was unquestionably the best person for the job. Notwithstanding some romanticised modern reconstructions there is no evidence that she actually fought in person in any of her battles, but she soon proved to be a military commander of considerable skill.

The policy of constructing defensible 'burghs' or fortresses may have been inspired originally by the Danish winter camps, but it had been developed by Alfred and Edward into a nationwide strategy. The burghs were intended to provide shelter for people and livestock against Viking raids, as well as channelling their movements, blocking fords and other strategic points, and generally making it more difficult for invading armies to manoeuvre across the country. Aethelflaed took advantage of her husband's victory at Tettenhall to turn this strategy into an offensive one, occupying one Danish-held town after another, and turning each into an English stronghold. In the summer of 913 she went 'with all the Mercians' to Tamworth, and fortified it. Offa's old capital had been a backwater since the establishment of the Danelaw had turned it into a disputed border town, but there is no record that Aethelflaed met with any opposition. Probably the Danes hurriedly evacuated it, if in fact they had ever had a garrison there. The Mercian army then moved on to Stafford, which they also took without difficulty. The Danes based at Leicester and Northampton were alarmed, but were unable to organise any effective retaliation, contenting themselves with a few raids in the regions of Luton and Hook Norton in the north of what is now Oxfordshire. These turned out to be a fiasco, and the Anglo-Saxon Chronicle tells how the local people turned out and attacked the once-dreaded Vikings, routing them and capturing most of their horses and weapons.

In 914 new Mercian burghs were founded at Warwick, and at Eddisbury near Chester. A raiding army led by Jarls Ohtar and Hroald sailed over from Brittany and ravaged the Lower Severn valley, but failed to distract Aetheflaed from her purpose. Instead the local levies from Hereford and Gloucester defeated them in battle, killed Hroald, and besieged the remainder in their camp until they agreed to provide hostages and leave the country. They then sailed downstream into the Bristol Channel where they tried twice to sneak ashore and pillage in Devon, but Edward had fortified the coast with numerous strongpoints and watchtowers, so they were detected on both occasions and their landing parties massacred. Those who escaped were forced to swim out to their ships and eventually to retreat to Ireland, greatly weakened by starvation.

Other Danish initiatives were no more successful. In 917 the occupiers of Leicester and Northampton attacked a new burgh which had been built by King Edward at Towcester, about eight miles south-west of Northampton. The garrison held out during a day of fierce fighting until reinforcements arrived, however, and the attackers withdrew. In the same year the East Anglians advanced west from Cambridge and built a fort at Tempsford, on the River Great Ouse downstream from Bedford, believing that from there they could more easily raid into central Mercia. However, the men of Bedford repulsed their attack, and soon afterwards Edward came up with a large army and stormed the Viking stronghold, killing or capturing the entire garrison.

Aethelflaed, meanwhile, 'took possession' of Derby, although on this occasion the Chronicle's brief notice hints at some serious resistance, since four of her favourite thegns were killed. Henry of Huntingdon says that although the town was held by 'a numerous garrison' the Vikings did not dare to come out and face the Mercians in the open, so most of the fighting took place around the main gate in the walls, where the four thegns met their deaths. Early in 918 Aethelflaed's armies closed in on Leicester, but by this time Viking resistance was crumbling throughout the country. The town surrendered without a fight, and shortly afterwards Aethelflaed received a delegation from the Danes in York, the centre of their power in Northumbria, offering her allegiance. What further conquests she might have achieved we can only speculate, because at this moment of triumph she died at Tamworth, 'twelve days before midsummer' in the year 918. She was buried beside her husband Aethelred at Saint Peter's Church in Gloucester.

Her death marks the end of the history of the Mercian Wars, because she was the last ruler of even a semi-independent Mercian state. The only candidate to succeed her was her daughter Aelfwynn, but she did not possess the experience and ability which had made her mother acceptable as a leader of warriors. She was quietly deposed by her uncle King Edward, who took her into Wessex where she disappears from history, probably into a nunnery. According to the Chronicle, 'all the nation of the land of Mercia which was formerly subject to Aethelflaed turned to him,' and from then on Mercia was to be ruled directly by the kings of Wessex, soon to be universally recognised as kings of England. Pro-Wessex though it is, there is no reason to believe that the Chronicle was wrong to suggest that the transfer of power was peaceful. The idea of nationhood had hardly been formulated at that time, and most men undoubtedly thought of their primary loyalty as being to an individual rather than a 'country'. With no native Mercian dynasty surviving, Edward was the obvious choice for their allegiance.

Under his leadership and that of his even more illustrious successor Athelstan, who reigned from 924 to 939, the rulers of Wessex were to unite the entire English people for the first time under a single king. The Mercians would continue to participate fully in this process. In 937 Athelstan crushed an alliance of Vikings and Scots at the Battle of Brunanburgh, celebrated by a poem inserted in the Anglo-Saxon Chronicle which tells how the Mercians, fighting alongside the West Saxons, 'refused hard hand-play to none', ending the day as masters of a field on which five kings, seven jarls and countless warriors of lesser rank among the enemy lay dead. Men such as these had not been beaten by the Vikings, nor 'conquered' by the West Saxons – despite the claim in an exaggerated eulogy of King Edmund inserted in the Chronicle in 942 – but had bravely defended their land through all its changes of fortune, and brought it as a respected partner into the new English kingdom.

Conclusion

It was the misfortune of the ancient royal line of Mercia that it ceased to produce great war leaders just at the time when the English people, gradually coalescing into a single nation under the pressure of the Viking invasions, needed them most. Hence a genealogical accident has led historians ever since to see Wessex as the true precursor of England, and to this day accounts of the English (and later British) monarchy still tend to begin with Alfred the Great. The most eminent of his predecessors – men such as Raedwald, Edwin, Penda, and even Offa himself – remain in relative obscurity. In the popular imagination they appear – if at all – as barbarian warlords, ruling over primitive kingdoms that just happened to have been located on what became English territory, but which had little in common with England as we know it today. And yet things might have turned out very differently.

If Offa had left behind a long-lived heir and a secure line of succession, or if Aethelflaed had been succeeded by the warlike son that the times seemed to require, the political centre of gravity might have remained in Mercia for much longer. It is even possible that if the Anglo-Saxons had been united sooner under Mercian leadership they might have been better able to resist both the Vikings and the Normans. It is hard to imagine an alternative history in which Tamworth or Lichfield became the capital of a united England – the economic dominance of the port of London would eventually have overshadowed all rival political centres in any case – but the role of the Mercian kings as the first to exercise real authority over the

Anglo-Saxons south of the Humber might have been more widely acknowledged.

Nevertheless, in the towns and villages which once witnessed the glory of this lost dynasty, there remains a tradition of its former eminence, and a quiet pride in its achievements. Of course these communities have fared differently over the years. Tamworth still proclaims itself the 'ancient capital of Mercia', and celebrates the fact in everything from street names to advertising posters. More soberly, Lichfield has functioned continuously as an ecclesiastical centre since the days of the conversion. The eighth-century 'Saint Chad Gospels', which is still carried in procession through the cathedral at Christmas and Easter just as it may have been when Offa heard mass in an earlier building on the site, is said to be the oldest book in the country still being used for its intended purpose. Brixworth is a growing commuter village just outside Northampton, but is well aware of the remarkable asset represented by its church, where an annual Brixworth Lecture is given by an expert in Anglo-Saxon studies. By contrast Seckington, a tiny hamlet situated in a surprisingly remote stretch of countryside east of Tamworth, pre-serves no hint that it was once the seat of kings. However, the hill on which All Saints Church now stands, probably the site of the royal hall where Aethelbald met his death, commands a spectacular view to the south very reminiscent of that from the height at Brixworth. Clearly these highly visible locations were favoured for the display of kingly power, as well as for their security against surprise. Though not a single battlefield of the Mercian Wars has been preserved or even precisely located, the landscape of Central England still has tales to tell of the men who first made it into a kingdom.

Bibliography

Main Primary Sources

The Anglo-Saxon Chronicles, trans. M. Swanton, London, 1996.

Asser, *Life of King Alfred*, trans. S. Keynes and M. Lapidge, London, 1983.

Bede, *A History of the English Church and People*, trans. L. Sherley-Price, Harmondsworth, 1955.

Beowulf, trans. M. Alexander, Harmondsworth, 1973.

English Historical Documents, Vol. 1, ed. D. Whitelock, London, 1968.

Nennius, *Historia Brittonum and Welsh Annals*, trans. J. Morris, London and Chichester, 1980.

The Chronicle of Henry of Huntingdon, trans. T. Forester, London, 1853.

William of Malmesbury, *Chronicle of the Kings of England*, trans. J. Giles, London, 1876.

Secondary Works

Abels, R., *Lordship and Military Obligation in Anglo-Saxon England*, London, 1988.

Alcock, L., *Economy, Society and Warfare Among the Britons and Saxons*, Cardiff, 1987.

Arnold, C., *An Archaeology of the Early Anglo-Saxon Kingdoms*, London and New York, 1988.

Bapty, I., review of Hill, D. and M. Worthington, *Offa's Dyke: History and Guide*, Stroud, 2003, at www.cpat.org.uk/offa.

Barley, M. W., in *Transactions of the Thoroton Society*, Vol. 60, Nottingham, 1952.

Bassett, S. (ed.), *The Origins of Anglo-Saxon Kingdoms*, Leicester, 1989.

Biddle, M. and B. Kjolbye-Biddle, 'Repton and the Vikings', *Antiquity*, Vol. 66, 1992.

Bradbury, J., *The Medieval Archer*, Woodbridge, 1985.

Breeze, A., 'The Battle of the Winwaed and the River Went', *Northern History*, Issue 41, 2004.

Brooke, C., *The Saxon and Norman Kings*, Glasgow, 1963.

Brooks, N., *Church, State and Access to Resources in Early Anglo-Saxon England*, Twentieth Brixworth Lecture, Brixworth, Northamptonshire, 2003.

Brown, M. and C. Farr (eds), *Mercia: An Anglo-Saxon Kingdom in Europe*, London, 2001.

Camden, W., *Britannia*, trans. P. Holland, London, 1610. (Published online at www.visionofbritain.org.uk.)

Carver, M., *Sutton Hoo: Burial Ground of Kings?*, London, 1998.

Chaney, W., *The Cult of Kingship in Anglo-Saxon England*, Manchester, 1970.

Clarkson, T., 'Locating Maserfelth', *The Heroic Age*, Issue 9, 2006.

Colgrave, B., *Felix's Life of Saint Guthlac*, Cambridge, 1956.

Dark, K., *Britain and the End of the Roman Empire*, Stroud, 2002.

Ellis Davidson, H., *The Sword in Anglo-Saxon England*, Woodbridge, 1994.

Finburg, H., *The Formation of England, 550 to 1042*, London, 1974.

Fleming, R., *Britain After Rome: The Fall and Rise, 400 to 1070*, London, 2010.

Fox, C., *Offa's Dyke*, Oxford, 1955.

Gardiner, J. (ed.), *Who's Who in British History*, London, 2000.

Gelling, M., *The West Midlands in the Early Middle Ages*, Leicester, 1992.

Griffith, P., *The Viking Art of War*, London, 1995.

Halsall, G., *War and Society in the Barbarian West*, London, 2003.

Harrison, M., *Anglo-Saxon Thegn, AD 449 to 1066*, Osprey Warrior Series 5, London, 1993.

Harting, J., *British Animals Extinct Within Historic Times*, London, 1880.

Hawkes, S. Chadwick (ed.), *Weapons and Warfare in Anglo-Saxon England*, Oxford University Committee for Archaeology Monograph 21, Oxford, 1989.

Heath, I., *Armies of the Dark Ages, 600 to 1066*, Worthing, 1980.

Higham, N., *The English Conquest: Gildas and Britain in the Fifth Century*, Manchester, 1994.

——, *An English Empire: Bede and the Early Anglo-Saxon Kings*, Manchester, 1995.

Hill, D. and M. Worthington, *Offa's Dyke: History and Guide*, Stroud, 2003. (Reviewed by I. Bapty at www.cpat.org.uk/offa.)

Hindley, G., *A Brief History of the Anglo-Saxons*, London, 2006.

Hollister, C. W., *Anglo-Saxon Military Institutions on the Eve of the Norman Conquest*, Oxford, 1962.

Hooke, D., *The Landscape of Anglo-Saxon Staffordshire: The Charter Evidence*, Keele, 1983.

——, *The Anglo-Saxon Landscape: The Kingdom of the Hwicce*, Manchester, 1985.

Jancey, E., *Saint Ethelbert, Patron Saint of Hereford Cathedral*, Hereford, 1994.

Jennings, J. C., 'The Writings of Prior Dominic of Evesham', *English Historical Review*, Vol. 77, 1962.

Jones, G., *A History of the Vikings*, London, 1968.

Kenyon, D., *The Origins of Lancashire*, Manchester, 1991.

Kirby, D., *The Earliest English Kings*, London, 1991.

Leahy, K. and R. Bland, *The Staffordshire Hoard*, London, 2009.

Loades, M., *Swords and Swordsmen*, Barnsley, 2010.

Lucy, S., *The Anglo-Saxon Way of Death*, Stroud, 2000.

McNeill, W., *Plagues and Peoples*, New York, 1976.

Myres, J., *The English Settlements*, Oxford, 1986.

Nicolle, D., *Carolingian Cavalryman, AD 768 to 987*, Osprey Warrior Series 96, Oxford, 2005.

North, A., 'Barbarians and Christians', in M. Coe et al., *Swords and Hilt Weapons*, London, 1989.

Oppenheimer, S., *The Origins of the British*, London, 2006.

189

Pollington, S., *The English Warrior from Earliest Times till 1066*, Frithgarth, 2001.

Prestwich, J., 'King Aethelhere and the Battle of the Winwaed', *English Historical Review*, Vol. 83, 1968.

Pryor, F., *Britain AD: A Quest for Arthur, England and the Anglo-Saxons*, London, 2004.

——, *Britain in the Middle Ages: An Archaeological History*, London, 2006.

Rackham, O., *The History of the Countryside*, London, 1986.

Revill, S., in *Transactions of the Thoroton Society*, Vol. 79, Nottingham, 1975.

Rowland, J., *Early Welsh Saga Poetry*, Cambridge, 1990.

Russell, M. and S. Laycock, *Unroman Britain*, Stroud, 2010.

Stenton, F., *Anglo-Saxon England*, Oxford, 1971.

Stephanus, E., 'Life of Saint Wilfred', in J. F. Webb, *Lives of the Saints*, London, 1965.

Stone, R., *Tamworth: A History*, Chichester, 2003.

Strickland, M. and R. Hardy, *The Great War Bow*, Stroud, 2005.

Sykes, B., *Blood of the Isles: Exploring the Genetic Roots of our Tribal History*, London, 2006.

Swanton, M., *The Spearheads of the Anglo-Saxon Settlements*, Leeds, 1973.

——, *Opening the Franks Casket*, Fourteenth Brixworth Lecture, Leicester, 1998.

Underwood, R., *Anglo-Saxon Weapons and Warfare*, Stroud, 1999.

Upton, C., *A History of Lichfield*, Chichester, 2001.

Walker, I., *Mercia and the Making of England*, Stroud, 2000.

Whitelock, D., *The Beginnings of English Society*, Harmondsworth, 1952.

Wood, M., *In Search of the Dark Ages*, London, 1981.

——, *Domesday: A Search for the Roots of England*, London, 1986.

Woodruffe, D., *The Life and Times of Alfred the Great*, London, 1974.

Yorke, B., *Kings and Kingdoms of Early Anglo-Saxon England*, London, 1990.

Zaluckyi, S., *Mercia: The Anglo-Saxon Kingdom of Central England*, Logaston, 2001.

Index

Note: No entries will be found for the major English kingdoms – Mercia, Wessex, Northumbria, East Anglia and Kent – as these would be too numerous to be helpful. Modern county names appear in the text only as rough guides to the location of places mentioned, so are not indexed except where they correspond to the smaller English kingdoms of the period such as Essex and Sussex.

191